HOW TO FORM YOUR OWN CORPORATION WITHOUT A LAWYER FOR UNDER $50.00

By Ted Nicholas

Complete with Tear-out Forms
Certificate of Incorporation
Minutes, By-Laws—
Everything that is needed

"This publication is designed to provide accurate and authoritative information in regard to the subject matter covered in it. It is sold with the understanding that the publisher is not engaged in rendering legal, accounting, or other professional service. If legal advice or other expert assistance is required, the services of a competent professional person should be sought." —From a Declaration of Principles jointly adopted by a Committee of the American Bar Association and a Committee of Publishers and Associations.

Published by

ENTERPRISE PUBLISHING, INC.
725 North Market Street
Wilmington, Delaware 19801
1-800-533-2665
Total Number of Copies in Print 875,000
Printed in the United States of America

ACKNOWLEDGMENTS

I'd like to thank my friend, Sylvan N. Levy, Jr. for his useful suggestions after spending many hours reviewing the manuscript.

Additionally, the entire staff of Enterprise Publishing, Inc. has been of enormous assistance in the preparation of this book.

More Acknowledgments

In connection with this writing, special acknowledgment is given the Corporation Department, Secretary of State's office in Dover, Delaware and capable staff.

In particular, I deeply appreciate the efforts of the Assistant Secretary of State, Mr. Richard H. Caldwell, for his personal assistance and helpful comments in the review of the contents of this book.

Since the first printing of the hardcover edition in January 1973, Robert Reed, Secretary of State, appointed by Governor Sherman Tribbitt, Mr. Grover Biddle, the Assistant Secretary of State and Mrs. Marie Shultie, Director, Corporation Department, and her staff, have been of enormous assistance in helping to process smoothly and efficiently the large volume of new corporations from all over the world that have been formed as a result of this book.

At the time of this printing, the present Secretary of State, Mr. Michael E. Harkins (and Jeffrey S. Lewis, Acting Assistant Secretary of State) appointed by Governor Michael N. Castle, continue with the fine work that has been historically done by the Corporation Department.

T.N.

A BRIEF HISTORY OF THE CORPORATION

Much of American law has its origin in England. The Corporation as a legal entity under English law dates back to the late 14th century. In the early 1600's, again in England, a number of joint stock associations were formed in an attempt to gain the same advantage as chartered corporations. In all contractual dealings, these companies were able to offer their stockholders liability protection. Investors in such companies were as a result put in a more favorable position than partners whose liabilities for corporate debts are unlimited.

Corporations have been a part of North America's history for over 300 years. The Massachusetts Bay Company was chartered in 1629 by Charles I of England. Its purpose was to colonize the area near Massachusetts Bay. Subsequently, in 1630, it founded the city of Boston. The Hudson Bay Company of Canada was chartered in 1670 and continues to operate trading posts there today.

During the early stages of the American Republic, it took a special act of a state legislature to grant a corporate charter to a business enterprise. The first state to permit incorporation under a general law was New York in 1811.

By 1900, nearly all the states had constitutional provisions forbidding the granting of corporate charters by legislators.

Delaware was the first state to ratify the U.S. Constitution in 1787. The Delaware General Corporation law was adopted in 1899. Prior to this time corporate charters were granted by an act of the legislature. It was the pioneer State in creating an attractive climate for free enterprise. Many of the corporations begun during America's great industrial revolution during the 1800's were chartered in Delaware. This friendly and accommodating atmosphere toward business enterprises still exists today. Low taxes, fast service, simplified requirements, and the Court of Chancery, the only separate business court system in the U.S., combine to attract both small one-man corporations as well as large corporations to Delaware. One-third of the companies listed on American and New York Stock Exchanges are chartered in Delaware.

Corporations in America in the early stages were burdened with sharp restrictions on longevity and size. Terms fixed to specific number of years, 20 to 50 years, were common. There were also ceilings an authorized capital. These and other limits were abandoned over a period of time.

In the 1700's a large part of world commerce was carried on by corporations. By the late 1800's corporations had multiplied enormously. Nearly every business owner that required capital, a union of large numbers of people or desired limited liability incorporated. The wealth and business holdings in the country to a great extent was and is controlled by them.

At present the States compete with each other to attract business to them. Some are more aggressive than others. This creates a healthy and unusual atmosphere. Many have attempted to model sections of their law on the General Corporation law of Delaware. However, while there are some similarities no State has been successful in achieving all Delaware's benefits.

Today, there are more than 2,000,000 active corporations. About 800,000 of these elected to be taxed like partnerships. According to the Wall Street Journal in excess of 50,000 new corporations are formed each month in North America.

As of this revised edition, this book is used by a measurable and growing number of them — 500 to 600 each month, or nearly 2% of all the corporations formed each month in the United States.

TABLE OF CONTENTS

Definition: A Corporation is an entity created through the act of filing a document by an individual or group, known as articles of or certificate of incorporation with a state agency known as "Corporation Department." This entity is recognized by law as a separate "person" existing in reality with limited liability, a separate tax status, the right to sue and be sued, the option of selling shares, and the capacity of succession.

"For many years, even decades, the Delaware General Corporation Law has been the pace-setter for American corporation statues. Indeed, viewed realistically, Delaware Corporation Law is national corporation law."

"The fact is that states cannot effectively exert controls and restrictions even over enterprises organized under their own corporation statutes. If they attempt to do so, enterprises merely incorporate in some other state with a more 'liberal' statute since the federal system permits individuals to incorporate wherever they wish in order to do business on a local, state, national, or international level."

> From book, The DELAWARE GENERAL
> CORPORATION LAW
>
> written by Ernest L. Folk, III, Professor of
> Law, University of Virginia and published
> for Corporation Service Company by
> Little, Brown and Company, Inc.
> 34 Beacon Street
> Boston, MA 02106 $47.50

"Anyone may so arrange his affairs that his taxes shall be as low as possible; He is not bound to choose that pattern which will best pay the Treasury; there is not even a patriotic duty to increase one's taxes."

Judge Learned Hand

FOREWORD

The experience of the author is as a businessman and business consultant.

This book enables the reader to incorporate at the lowest possible cost. The forms that are necessary are in tear-out type and are complete with instructions.

The author is a principal in The Company Corporation. This corporation provides various low cost services to persons who form a corporation (See Section VII).

Lawyer's fees for incorporating range from $300 to $3,000 or more. The system enables anyone in the United States to form a corporation without a lawyer at the lowest possible cost, and includes other money saving and tax saving ideas.

A little known fact is that in many states an individual can legally incorporate without the services of a lawyer. Lawyers provide important professional services to their clients. However, incorporation is a relatively simple task that does not require professional services. There are some lawyers who would like to charge lower fees for forming a corporation. State Bar Associations, however, provide recommended fee schedules for lawyers who do not like to go against these recommendations. Forming a corporation usually involves minimum legal fees of at least $300. This fee varies in accordance with the schedule or recommended fees of a particular State Bar Association. Average fees charged by lawyers tend to be higher than the recommended minimum.

Before this book was written, it was difficult for an individual to incorporate without a lawyer. The reason for this is that there was no publication on the matter written in everyday English. In addition, companies that assist individuals in forming a corporation work only through a lawyer who prepares the corporate documents. Legal fees for incorporation heretofore, were almost completely unavoidable.

Delaware is emphasized as the state in which to incorporate. Regardless of where a person lives or has a business, this book enables a person to incorporate and take advantage of Delaware Corporate Laws. In Delaware, anyone can form a corporation as long as he completes the forms provided for that purpose himself. The reason for this can be found in Section II.

Delaware is the State of Incorporation for over 184,000 corporations. They range from small one man operations, to the largest ones in the United States. Because of the advantages to corporations of Delaware Corporate Laws, more than one-third of all corporations listed on the American and New York Stock Exchange are Delaware corporations. This is a much higher percentage than any other state.

The biggest percentage of the corporations formed in Delaware are headquartered in other states. The individuals who own these corporations almost never visit the state.

There are over twenty companies whose function is to act as "Registered Agent" and provide services including a Delaware mailing address for the corporations formed in Delaware.

In most cases, the needs of an individual or company who wishes to incorporate involve a simple corporate structure. The goal of this book is directed toward the simplest and lowest cost method of forming a corporation. A person with a business of any type or size that wishes to incorporate and engage in any business endeavor anywhere in the United States can beneficially utilize the elements contained herein.

As of this edition the count of new corporations that have been formed by using this book has reached many thousands. Owners of these corporations reside in all 50 of the United States as well as in several other countries throughout the world.

Prices and fees quoted in this book may be increased without notice by the various States and other bodies, and should only be used as a guide.

ADVANTAGES OF INCORPORATING

SECTION I

Before one decides whether or not to incorporate, it is wise to review other alternatives.

There are two other fundamental ways to operate a business, individual proprietorship and partnership. Both have similar advantages and disadvantages. The main advantage is that they are slightly less expensive to start, since there are no incorporating fees. They are also a bit less formal.

In a corporation, periodic meetings and minutes of meetings should be kept. This is a simple routine task. (See Section XXI)

ADVANTAGES OF PARTNERSHIPS AND PROPRIETORSHIPS

1. Somewhat lower cost to organize since there are no incorporating fees.
2. Less formality in record keeping.
3. The owners file one tax return.
4. Owners can deduct losses that might be incurred during the early life of a business from other personal income.
5. The limit of tax deductible contributions to "Keogh" type pension and profit sharing plans has been increased to $30,000. This has reduced the tax advantage of benefit plans previously available to a corporation.
6. Profits of a partnership, unlike dividends paid by a corporation are not subject to a second Federal income tax when distributed to the owners. However, whether this is an advantage, taxwise, depends on certain other factors, namely:
    a. The individual tax brackets of the owners as compared with that of the corporation.
    b. The extent to which double taxation of earnings of the corporation is eliminated by deductible salaries paid to owners and by retention of earnings in surplus.

SOME OF THE MAIN DISADVANTAGES OF PROPRIETORSHIPS AND PARTNERSHIPS ARE:

1. Unlimited personal liability. The owners are personally liable for all debts and judgments against the business, including liability in case of failure or other disaster.
2. In a partnership, each member can bind the other so that one partner can cause the other to be personally liable.
3. If the owner(s) dies or becomes incapacitated, the business often comes to a standstill.
4. The owner(s) do not have the full tax benefits of the tax deductible plans including pension and profit sharing that are available to a corporation.

THE ADVANTAGES OF INCORPORATING INCLUDE:

1. The personal liability of the founders is limited to the amount of money put into the corporation (with the exception of unpaid taxes).
2. If a business owner wishes to raise capital, a corporation is more attractive to investors who can purchase shares of stock in it for purposes of raising capital.
3. A corporation does not pay tax on monies it receives in exchange for its stock.

3

4. There are many more tax options available to corporations than to proprietorships or partnerships. One can set up pension, profit sharing, stock option plans that are favorable to the owners of the corporation.

5. A corporation can be continued more easily in the event of the death of its owners or principals.

6. Shares of a corporation can easily be distributed to family members.

7. The owners (stockholders) of a corporation that is discontinued due to its being unsuccessful can have all the advantages of being incorporated, yet be able to deduct up to $50,000 on an individual tax return or $100,000 on a joint return of money invested in the corporation from personal income. (See Section XV)

8. The owner(s), stockholders, of a corporation can operate with all the advantages of a corporation, yet be taxed on personal income tax rates if this option provides a tax advantage. (See Section XVI)

9. Owners can quickly transfer their ownership interest represented by shares of stock, without the corporation dissolving.

10. The corporation's capital can be expanded by issuing and selling additional shares of stock.

11. Shares of stock can be used for estate and family planning.

12. The corporation can ease the tax burden of its stockholders by accumulating its earnings. This is providing the accumulation is not unreasonable and is for a business purpose.

13. It is a separate legal "being," separate and apart from its owner(s) (stockholders). It can sue and be sued and can enter into contracts.

14. A corporation may own shares in another corporation and receive dividends, 80% of which are tax free.

15. A corporation's Federal Income Tax Rates may be lower than the owner's individual tax rates, especially for a company with taxable income in the $28,000 to $100,000 range. Beginning in July 1987 the Income Tax Rates on companies are as follows:

Taxable Income	Rate of Tax
Up to $50,000	15%
$50,000—$75,000	25%
Over $75,000	34%

DISADVANTAGES OF INCORPORATING INCLUDE:

1. The owners of a corporation file two tax returns, individual and corporate. This may require added time and accounting expense. (The owner of a proprietorship files one return; a member of a partnership files two.)

2. If the net taxable income of a business is substantial, i.e. $75,000 or more, there may not be tax advantages. (However, in businesses where there is personal liability on the part of the owners, it may be desirable to incorporate even if the income is modest.)

3. Maintaining the corporate records may require added time. (See corporate forms, Section XXI.)

4. If debt financing is obtained by a corporation, i.e., a loan from a bank, the fund source may require the personal guarantee by the owner(s) thereby eliminating the limited liability advantage of a corporation at least to the extent of the loan.

   NOTE: Probably the biggest single disadvantage to incorporating prior to the publication of this book, was the high initial cost.

REASONS FOR INCORPORATING IN DELAWARE

SECTION II

The advantages of incorporating in Delaware are:

1. There is *no* minimum capital requirement. A corporation can be organized with *zero* capital, if desired. Many states require that a corporation have at least $1,000 in capital.

2. *One* person can hold the offices of President, Treasurer, and Secretary, and be all the directors. Many states require at least three officers and/or directors. Therefore, there is no need to bring other persons into a Delaware Corporation if the owner(s) does not desire it.

3. There is an established body of laws relevant to corporations that have been tested in the Delaware courts over the years. In the event of any legal matters that involve Delaware courts there is, therefore, a high degree of predictability of the outcome of any legal proceedings based on past history and experience. This can be meaningful to investors in a corporation. The Court of Chancery in Delaware is the only separate business court system in the United States, and has a long record of pro-management decisions.

4. There is no corporation income tax for any corporations that are formed in Delaware but who do not do business in the state.

5. The Franchise Tax on corporations compares favorably with any other state.

6. Shares of stock owned by a person outside the state are not subject to any Delaware taxes.

7. A person can operate as the owner of a Delaware corporation anonymously if desired. (See Section XIV.)

8. One can form a corporation by mail and never visit the state, even to conduct Annual Meetings. Meetings can be held anywhere, at the option of the directors.

9. The Delaware Corporation Department welcomes new corporations and is organized to process them the same day they are received.

10. Delaware is the friendliest state to corporations. The reason is that the state depends on its corporation department as a prime source of revenue. The corporation revenue is exceeded by income taxes. The state, therefore, depends on attracting a high volume of corporations. It has, historically, kept its laws and fees relevant to corporations favorable and at a low cost.

11. There is no Inheritance Tax on shares of stock held by non-residents. These shares are taxed only in the state of residence of the owners of the corporation.

12. Director(s) may fix a sales price on any stock that the corporation issues and wishes to sell.

13. Stockholders, directors, and/or committee members may act by unanimous written consent in lieu of formal meetings.

14. Director(s) may determine what part of consideration received for stock is capital.

15. Corporations can pay dividends out of profits as well as surplus.

16. Corporations can hold stocks, bonds, or securities of other corporations, real and personal property, within or without the state, without limitation as to amount.

17. Corporations may purchase shares of its own stock and hold, sell and transfer them.

18. Corporations may conduct different kinds of business in combination. If the corporate documents filed with Delaware have the broadest type "purpose clause" as outlined in this book, any business activity of any kind may be conducted. More than one type of business

can be conducted by the same corporation without any changes in the documents filed with the state.

19. Corporations have perpetual existence (unless specified in its Certificate of Incorporation).

20. The director(s) has power to make or alter by-laws.

21. Stockholder liability is limited to stock held in the corporation (with exception of taxes and assuming the business is conducted in a legal manner).

22. Only one person acting as the incorporator is required, whereas many states require three.

23. Director(s) personal liability is either entirely eliminated or strictly limited under a new law passed in 1986 (Section 102(b)(7), Title 8 of the Delaware Code).

24. Recent legislation has provided a balance between the benefits of an unfettered market for corporate shares and the well documented and judicially recognized need to limit abusive takeover tactics.

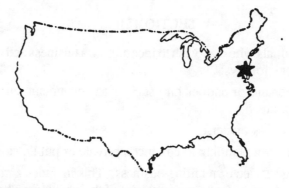

Percentage of Corporations Listed on the New York and American Stock Exchanges Which are Incorporated in The Top Ten States.

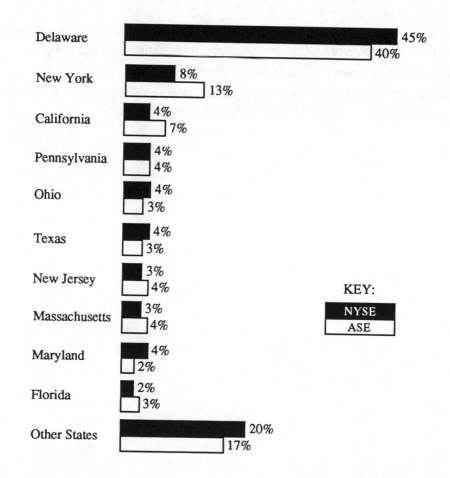

State	NYSE	ASE
Delaware	45%	40%
New York	8%	13%
California	4%	7%
Pennsylvania	4%	4%
Ohio	4%	3%
Texas	4%	3%
New Jersey	3%	4%
Massachusetts	3%	4%
Maryland	4%	2%
Florida	2%	3%
Other States	20%	17%

KEY:
NYSE
ASE

TYPES OF SITUATIONS WHERE INDIVIDUALS
MIGHT WISH TO INCORPORATE

SECTION III

A few examples of individuals who may wish to incorporate a business activity or profession planned or presently in operation are as follows:

1. A professional person (or partnership) such as an accountant, engineer, physician, dentist, architect, lawyer, etc.

2. A franchised business owner.

3. A person or company planning to conduct a private or public stock offering.

4. A manufacturing service or retailing business. This includes a manufacturer's representative, a distributor (many of whom operate out of their homes). The list of types of situations include, but are not limited to: any type of retail operation, gas station, publishing, mail order operation, restaurant, beauty shop, loan company, etc.

5. A personal real estate investment such as an apartment building, store, or any commercial building project.

6. A business endeavor that would involve the ownership of one or more shareholders (sometimes called partners).

7. An activity or organization that is organized for non-profit purposes; such as a foundation association, charitable organization, volunteer organization or fire company.

8. A company which invests in securities or other companies.

It often makes good sense both from a tax and personal liability standpoint, for certain interests of an individual, such as a real estate investment, to be incorporated separately.

CERTIFICATE OF INCORPORATION

SECTION IV

When a Delaware corporation is formed, a Certificate of Incorporation is filed with the Secretary of State's office and with the Recorder of Deeds. It is also necessary to have minutes of the first Director's Meeting, By-Laws of the corporation, stock certificates and the corporate seal (forms for everything except stock certificates and corporate seal are supplied in this book).

Any person or his Registered Agent (See Section VI) can file the Certificate of Incorporation.

An individual or his Registered Agent can also arrange to provide the corporation with a Delaware address. Preparation of minutes of the first director's meeting, by-laws, stock certificates and corporate seal all can be ordered and completed by the person incorporating. Minutes and by-laws in standard form can be removed from this book and used for this purpose. A complete sample specimen and blank certificate of corporation are shown in Section V. Forms for by-laws and minutes are in Section XXI.

A very important element of the certificate is the Purpose Clause in paragraph three. The broadest clause enabling the corporation to engage in any business activity is used in this book. No matter what businesses the corporation engages in, this clause need not be changed. The broadest powers are given to the director(s) and officer(s). The only types of corporations to which this clause does not apply are institutions, schools, insurance companies, professional corporations, and banks.

3,000 shares of stock, which is the maximum number for the minimum state fee, are used in the sample specimen. This premise takes into consideration the Annual Corporate Franchise Fee which is only $30 for 3,000 shares. If this number of shares *or any lesser number* is selected initially as the number authorized by the corporation, it can easily be changed at any time if more shares are to be issued later. More shares, stock splits or a new capital structure involve only a simple form to be filed with the state. A schedule showing the fees for these types of changes is available from the Secretary of State, Dover, Delaware. A Delaware Registered Agent can file the forms involving these changes or they can be filed by an individual residing anywhere in the United States.

FORMING THE CORPORATION WITHOUT ENGAGING A REGISTERED AGENT

SECTION V

Any person can form a Delaware corporation. The owner(s) never has to visit the state. Annual meetings may be held anywhere.

Below is the least costly way to accomplish the incorporation. (This approach, while the least costly, does not include the benefits of the services a registered agent can provide.)

The following are the steps involved:

1. Established a street mailing address in Delaware. This can be a private home or office. (Without engaging a registered agent's services, to provide assistance, this is usually the most difficult problem to solve.) See Section VI.

2. Decide on whether to form a regular corporation or close corporation. (See Section V-A.) Complete the blank certificate of incorporation on the following pages, using the same format on the succeeding page. The language in this certificate has been prepared by the Secretary of State, Dover, Delaware. Be sure to fill in the name and address of one incorporator who resides in any state.

   Send two copies of this certificate to the Secretary of State, Corporation Department, Townsend Building, Dover, Delaware 19901. Include a check in the amount of $50.00 which is the total cost of the incorporation. (This fee breaks down as follows: $25 for filing, receiving and indexing; $15 is the minimum State filing fee; and $10.00 for a certified copy.)

   If the corporate name you pick is not available you will be notified. Otherwise you will receive notice of the date that your corporation has been filed.

3. When you receive one certified copy of the certificate of incorporation plus a receipted bill from the State, this copy should then be filed with the Recorder of Deeds office in the county where the street mailing address of the Corporation is located. There are three counties in Delaware. The addresses for the Recorder of Deeds offices in the three counties are as follows:

   Kent County — County Courthouse, Dover, Delaware 19901

   Sussex County — Box 505, Georgetown, Delaware 19947

   New Castle County — 800 French Street, Wilmington, Delaware 19801

   Enclose a check for $21.00* (The charge is $9.00 *per page* submitted, minimum $18.00 to record a one page certificate and certification page, plus a $3.00 document recording fee. Conventional certificates prepared and typed on legal size paper are from four to ten pages, costing the person filing from $39.00 to $93.00. This is the reason that all the certificates of incorporation except the non-stock are printed on *one page* and are available from The Company Corporation.)

   In some states, other than Delaware, a similar incorporation procedure applies. If a reader is interested for any reason in forming a non-Delaware corporation, he can obtain specific information by writing to the Corporation Department, Secretary of State in any state. However, no state has all the benefits of incorporating in Delaware.

---

* *Applies to New Castle County only.*

Standard forms are provided in Section XXI for by-laws and minutes of the first meeting.

There are also legal stationery companies that can supply a complete kit of the above forms, at a cost ranging from $45 to $70. A corporate seal and stock certificates cost $20 to $30.

The Company Corporation provides a "kit" including a corporate seal, stock certificates, forms for minutes for Section 1244 of the Internal Revenue Code (See Section VII) for $44.95, plus $5.00 for U.P.S. delivery.

If you prefer to engage a registered agent to act in your behalf, such services can easily be obtained. (See Section VI)

CERTIFICATE OF INCORPORATION

of

JOHN DOE, INC.

FIRST: The name of this corporation is __(Repeat name exactly as above)__

JOHN DOE, INC.

SECOND. Its registered office in the State of Delaware is to be located at __725 Market Street__ in the __City of Wilmington__, County of __New Castle__.

The registered agent in charge thereof is __(Name and address of your registered agent)__

The Company Corporation at __same as above__

THIRD. The nature of the business and, the objects and purposes to be transacted, promoted and carried on, are to do any or all the things herein mentioned, as fully and to the same extent as natural persons might or could do, and in any part of the world, viz:

"The purpose of the corporation is to engage in any lawful act or activity for which corporations may be organized under the General Corporation Law of Delaware."

FOURTH. The amount of the total authorized capital stock of this corporation is __3,000__ share of __no__ Par Value.

FIFTH. The name and mailing address of the incorporator is as follows:

NAME: ADDRESS:

(Leave blank if using The Company Corporation as agent, otherwise, your name and address)

SIXTH. The powers of the incorporator are to terminate upon filing of the certificate of incorporation, and the name(s) and mailing address(es) of persons who are to serve as director(s) until the first annual meeting of stockholders or until their successors are elected and qualify are as follow:

Name and address of director(s)

John Doe, 1 Main Street, Atlantis, CA.   Fill in name(s)
Jane Doe, 1 Main Street, Atlantis, CA.   and address(es)

SEVENTH. The Directors shall have power to make and to alter or amend the By-Laws; to fix the amount to be reserved as working capital, and to authorize and cause to be executed, mortgages and liens without limit as to the amount, upon the property and franchise of the Corporation.

With the consent in writing, and pursuant to a vote of the holders of majority of the capital stock issued and outstanding, the Directors shall have the authority to dispose, in any manner, of the whole property of this corporation.

The By-Laws shall determine whether and to what extent the accounts and books of this corporation, or any of them shall be open to the inspection of the stockholders; and no stockholder shall have any right of inspecting any account, or book or document of this Corporation, except as conferred by the law or the By-Laws, or by resolution of the stockholders.

The stockholders and directors shall have power to hold their meetings and keep the books, documents and papers of the Corporation outside of the State of Delaware, at such places as may be from time to time designated by the By-Laws or by resolution of the stockholders or directors, except as otherwise required by the laws of Delaware.

It is the intention that the objects, purposes and powers specified in the Third paragraph hereof shall, except where otherwise specified in said paragraph, be nowise limited or restricted by reference to or inference from the terms of any other clause or paragraph in this certificate of incorporation, but that the objects, purposes and powers specified in the Third paragraph and in each of the clauses or paragraphs of this charter shall be regarded as independent objects, purposes and powers.

EIGHTH. Directors of the corporation shall not be liable to either the corporation or its stockholders for monetary damages for a breach of fiduciary duties unless the breach involves: (1) a director's duty of loyalty to the corporation or its stockholders; (2) acts or omissions not in good faith or which involve intentional misconduct or a knowing violation of law; (3) liability for unlawful payments of dividends or unlawful stock purchases or redemption by the corporation; or (4) a transaction from which the director derived an improper personal benefit.

I, THE UNDERSIGNED, for the purpose of forming a Corporation under the laws of the State of Delaware, do make, file and record this Certificate and do certify that the facts herein are true; and I have accordingly hereunto set my hand.

DATED AT: _____

State of _____

County of _____

(Leave blank unless you are incorporator)

John Doe

(Signature of person or officer of corporation named in Fifth Article.)

(Leave blank if using The Company Corporation.)

CERTIFICATE OF INCORPORATION
of

_____

FIRST: The name of this corporation is_____

_____

SECOND. Its registered office in the State of Delaware is to be located at _____
in the _____, County of _____
The registered agent in charge thereof is_____
_____ at _____

THIRD. The nature of the business and, the objects and purposes to be transacted, promoted and carried on, are to do any or all the things herein mentioned, as fully and to the same extent as natural persons might or could do, and in any part of the world, viz:

"The purpose of the corporation is to engage in any lawful act or activity for which corporations may be organized under the General Corporation Law of Delaware."

FOURTH. The amount of the total authorized capital stock of this corporation is_____
_____ share of_____Par Value.

FIFTH. The name and mailing address of the incorporator is as follows:

NAME: ADDRESS:

_____   _____

SIXTH. The powers of the incorporator are to terminate upon filing of the certificate of incorporation, and the name(s) and mailing address(es) of persons who are to serve as director(s) until the first annual meeting of stockholders or until their successors are elected and qualify are as follow:

Name and address of director(s)

Fill in name(s)
and address(es)

SEVENTH. The Directors shall have power to make and to alter or amend the By-Laws; to fix the amount to be reserved as working capital, and to authorize and cause to be executed, mortgages and liens without limit as to the amount, upon the property and franchise of the Corporation.

With the consent in writing, and pursuant to a vote of the holders of majority of the capital stock issued and outstanding, the Directors shall have the authority to dispose, in any manner, of the whole property of this corporation.

The By-Laws shall determine whether and to what extent the accounts and books of this corporation, or any of them shall be open to the inspection of the stockholders; and no stockholder shall have any right of inspecting any account, or book or document of this Corporation, except as conferred by the law or the By-Laws, or by resolution of the stockholders.

The stockholders and directors shall have power to hold their meetings and keep the books, documents and papers of the Corporation outside of the State of Delaware, at such places as may be from time to time designated by the By-Laws or by resolution of the stockholders or directors, except as otherwise required by the laws of Delaware.

It is the intention that the objects, purposes and powers specified in the Third paragraph hereof shall, except where otherwise specified in said paragraph, be nowise limited or restricted by reference to or inference from the terms of any other clause or paragraph in this certificate of incorporation, but that the objects, purposes and powers specified in the Third paragraph and in each of the clauses or paragraphs of this charter shall be regarded as independent objects, purposes and powers.

EIGHTH. Directors of the corporation shall not be liable to either the corporation or its stockholders for monetary damages for a breach of fiduciary duties unless the breach involves: (1) a director's duty of loyalty to the corporation or its stockholders; (2) acts or omissions not in good faith or which involve intentional misconduct or a knowing violation of law; (3) liability for unlawful payments of dividends or unlawful stock purchases or redemption by the corporation; or (4) a transaction from which the director derived an improper personal benefit.

I, THE UNDERSIGNED, for the purpose of forming a Corporation under the laws of the State of Delaware, do make, file and record this Certificate and do certify that the facts herein are true; and I have accordingly hereunto set my hand.

DATED AT:_____

State of_____

County of_____

_____

CERTIFICATE OF INCORPORATION
of

_____

FIRST: The name of this corporation is _____

_____

SECOND. Its registered office in the State of Delaware is to be located at _____

in the _____, County of _____

The registered agent in charge thereof is_____

_____ at _____

THIRD. The nature of the business and, the objects and purposes to be transacted, promoted and carried on, are to do any or all the things herein mentioned, as fully and to the same extent as natural persons might or could do, and in any part of the world, viz:

"The purpose of the corporation is to engage in any lawful act or activity for which corporations may be organized under the General Corporation Law of Delaware."

FOURTH. The amount of the total authorized capital stock of this corporation is_____

_____ share of_____Par Value.

FIFTH. The name and mailing address of the incorporator is as follows:

NAME: ADDRESS:

_____   _____

SIXTH. The powers of the incorporator are to terminate upon filing of the certificate of incorporation, and the name(s) and mailing address(es) of persons who are to serve as director(s) until the first annual meeting of stockholders or until their successors are elected and qualify are as follow:

Name and address of director(s)

Fill in name(s)

and address(es)

SEVENTH. The Directors shall have power to make and to alter or amend the By-Laws; to fix the amount to be reserved as working capital, and to authorize and cause to be executed, mortgages and liens without limit as to the amount, upon the property and franchise of the Corporation.

With the consent in writing, and pursuant to a vote of the holders of majority of the capital stock issued and outstanding, the Directors shall have the authority to dispose, in any manner, of the whole property of this corporation.

The By-Laws shall determine whether and to what extent the accounts and books of this corporation, or any of them shall be open to the inspection of the stockholders; and no stockholder shall have any right of inspecting any account, or book or document of this Corporation, except as conferred by the law or the By-Laws, or by resolution of the stockholders.

The stockholders and directors shall have power to hold their meetings and keep the books, documents and papers of the Corporation outside of the State of Delaware, at such places as may be from time to time designated by the By-Laws or by resolution of the stockholders or directors, except as otherwise required by the laws of Delaware.

It is the intention that the objects, purposes and powers specified in the Third paragraph hereof shall, except where otherwise specified in said paragraph, be nowise limited or restricted by reference to or inference from the terms of any other clause or paragraph in this certificate of incorporation, but that the objects, purposes and powers specified in the Third paragraph and in each of the clauses or paragraphs of this charter shall be regarded as independent objects, purposes and powers.

EIGHTH. Directors of the corporation shall not be liable to either the corporation or its stockholders for monetary damages for a breach of fiduciary duties unless the breach involves: (1) a director's duty of loyalty to the corporation or its stockholders; (2) acts or omissions not in good faith or which involve intentional misconduct or a knowing violation of law; (3) liability for unlawful payments of dividends or unlawful stock purchases or redemption by the corporation; or (4) a transaction from which the director derived an improper personal benefit.

I, THE UNDERSIGNED, for the purpose of forming a Corporation under the laws of the State of Delaware, do make, file and record this Certificate and do certify that the facts herein are true; and I have accordingly hereunto set my hand.

DATED AT:_____

State of_____

County of_____

_____

A CLOSE CORPORATION

SECTION V-A

A close corporation is a corporation whose Certificate of Incorporation contains the basic elements contained in a standard Delaware corporation and, in addition, provides that:

1. All the corporation's issued stock shall be held by not more than a specified number of persons, not exceeding thirty.

2. All the issued stock shall be subject to one or more restrictions on transfer. The most widely used restriction is one which obligates a shareholder to offer to the corporation or other holders of shares of the corporation a prior opportunity to be exercised within a reasonable time to acquire the restricted securities.

Sometimes other restrictions are included in the Certificate of Incorporation which:

A. Obligate the corporation for any holder of shares of the corporation to purchase the shares which are the subject of an agreement regarding the purchase and sale of the restricted shares.

B. Require the corporation or shareholders of the corporation to consent to any proposed transfer of the restricted shares; or

C. Prohibit the transfer of restricted shares to designated persons or classes of persons if such designation is not unreasonable.

D. Any restriction on the transfer of shares of a corporation for the purpose of maintaining its status as an electing small business corporation under Subchapter "S" of the Internal Revenue Code is presumed to be for a reasonable purpose.

E. Another unique feature is that the certificate of incorporation of a close corporation may provide that the business of the corporation shall be managed by the stockholders. No directors need be elected so that there are no directors meetings necessary. This provision has the effect of eliminating the formality of having directors meetings. Under this feature, the shareholders of the corporation have the powers and responsibilities that directors would normally have.

A close corporation is not permitted to make a "public" offering of its shares within the meaning of the Securities Act of 1933.

If a person who is running a corporation wishes to limit shareholders in number and who also wishes that he and/or other shareholders to have the first opportunity to buy shares from a selling shareholder, a close corporation is the ideal type of form. This first option to buy shares of stock can be the key to preventing undesirable persons to become shareholders in a corporation.

An existing Delaware corporation can also elect to be a close corporation if two-thirds of the shareholders vote in favor of it. An amendment to this effect is filed with the Secretary of State in Dover, Delaware.

A close corporation can change its status to a regular or "open" corporation by filing a certificate of amendment with the Secretary of State.

On the following pages is a specimen copy and blank certificates that can be completed should a person wish to form a close corporation. It contains the provisions referred to in paragraphs 1, 2, and E.

As with other Delaware corporations, the certificate of incorporation can be filed using any address initially. However, it is preferable to have these filed through a registered agent since a Delaware mailing address is necessary.

19

CERTIFICATE OF INCORPORATION
of

<u>ABC Corporation</u>

A CLOSE CORPORATION

FIRST: The name of this corporation is <u>(Repeat proposed name here)</u>

<u>ABC Corporation</u>

SECOND: Its registered office in the State of Delaware is to be located at <u> </u>

<u>725 Market Street, City of Wilmington</u>

County of <u>New Castle</u> . The registered agent in charge thereof is:

<u>The Company Corporation</u>

<u> </u> address "same as above".

THIRD: The nature of the business and the objects and purposes proposed to be transacted, promoted and carried on, are to engage in any lawful act or activity for which cororations may be organized under the General Corporation Law of Delaware.

FOURTH: The amount of total authorized capital stock of the corporation is divided into:

<u>(# of shares desired) i.e.3000</u> shares of <u>No-par value (unless desire to establish a par value)</u>.

FIFTH: The name and mailing address of the incorporator is:

(Leave blank if using The Company Corporation as agent, otherwise your name and address)

SIXTH: The powers of the incorporator are to terminate upon filing of the Certificate of Incorporation, and the name(s) and mailing address(es) of the persons who are to serve as director(s) until the first annual meeting of stockholders or until their successors are elected are as follows:

<u>John Doe, 1 Main Street, Atlantis, Ca.</u>

SEVENTH: All of the corporation's issued stock, exclusive of treasury shares, shall be held of record by not more than thirty (30) persons.

EIGHTH: All of the issued stock of all classes shall be subject to the following restriction on transfer permitted by Section 202 of the General Corporation Law.

Each stockholder shall offer to the Corporation or to other stockholders of the corporation a thirty (30) day "first refusal" option to purchase his stock should he elect to sell his stock.

NINTH: The corporation shall make no offering of any of its stock of any class which would constitute a "public offering" within the meaning of the United States Securities Act of 1933, as it may be amended from time to time.

TENTH: Directors of the corporation shall not be liable to either the corporation or its stockholders for monetary damages for a breach of fiduciary duties unless the breach involves: (1) a director's duty of loyalty to the corporation or its stockholders; (2) acts or omissions not in good faith or which involve intentional misconduct or a knowing violation of law; (3) liability for unlawful payments of dividends or unlawful stock purchases or redemption by the corporation; or (4) a transaction from which the director derived an improper personal benefit.

I, THE UNDERSIGNED, for the purpose of forming a corporation under the laws of the State of Delaware, do make, file and record this certificate, and do certify that the facts herein stated are true; and I have accordingly hereunto set my hand.

DATED AT: <u> </u>

<u>*John Doe*</u>

(Signature of person or officer of corporation named in Fifth Article.)

(Leave blank if using The Company Corporation.)

CERTIFICATE OF INCORPORATION
of

_____

A CLOSE CORPORATION

FIRST: The name of this corporation is _____

_____

SECOND: Its registered office in the State of Delaware is to be located at _____

_____

County of_____ . The registered agent in charge thereof is:

_____

_____ address "same as above".

THIRD: The nature of the business and the objects and purposes proposed to be transacted, promoted and carried on, are to engage in any lawful act or activity for which cororations may be organized under the General Corporation Law of Delaware.

FOURTH: The amount of total authorized capital stock of the corporation is divided into:

_____ shares of _____

FIFTH: The name and mailing address of the incorporator is:

SIXTH: The powers of the incorporator are to terminate upon filing of the Certificate of Incorporation, and the name(s) and mailing address(es) of the persons who are to serve as director(s) until the first annual meeting of stockholders or until their successors are elected are as follows:

SEVENTH: All of the corporation's issued stock, exclusive of treasury shares, shall be held of record by not more than thirty (30) persons.

EIGHTH: All of the issued stock of all classes shall be subject to the following restriction on transfer permitted by Section 202 of the General Corporation Law.

Each stockholder shall offer to the Corporation or to other stockholders of the corporation a thirty (30) day "first refusal" option to purchase his stock should he elect to sell his stock.

NINTH: The corporation shall make no offering of any of its stock of any class which would constitute a "public offering" within the meaning of the United States Securities Act of 1933, as it may be amended from time to time.

TENTH: Directors of the corporation shall not be liable to either the corporation or its stockholders for monetary damages for a breach of fiduciary duties unless the breach involves: (1) a director's duty of loyalty to the corporation or its stockholders; (2) acts or omissions not in good faith or which involve intentional misconduct or a knowing violation of law; (3) liability for unlawful payments of dividends or unlawful stock purchases or redemption by the corporation; or (4) a transaction from which the director derived an improper personal benefit.

I, THE UNDERSIGNED, for the purpose of forming a corporation under the laws of the State of Delaware, do make, file and record this certificate, and do certify that the facts herein stated are true; and I have accordingly hereunto set my hand.

DATED AT:_____

_____

CERTIFICATE OF INCORPORATION
of

_____

A CLOSE CORPORATION

FIRST: The name of this corporation is _____

_____

SECOND: Its registered office in the State of Delaware is to be located at _____

_____

County of_____ . The registered agent in charge thereof is:

_____

_____ address "same as above".

THIRD: The nature of the business and the objects and purposes proposed to be transacted, promoted and carried on, are to engage in any lawful act or activity for which cororations may be organized under the General Corporation Law of Delaware.

FOURTH: The amount of total authorized capital stock of the corporation is divided into:

_____ shares of _____

FIFTH: The name and mailing address of the incorporator is:

SIXTH: The powers of the incorporator are to terminate upon filing of the Certificate of Incorporation, and the name(s) and mailing address(es) of the persons who are to serve as director(s) until the first annual meeting of stockholders or until their successors are elected are as follows:

SEVENTH: All of the corporation's issued stock, exclusive of treasury shares, shall be held of record by not more than thirty (30) persons.

EIGHTH: All of the issued stock of all classes shall be subject to the following restriction on transfer permitted by Section 202 of the General Corporation Law.

Each stockholder shall offer to the Corporation or to other stockholders of the corporation a thirty (30) day "first refusal" option to purchase his stock should he elect to sell his stock.

NINTH: The corporation shall make no offering of any of its stock of any class which would constitute a "public offering" within the meaning of the United States Securities Act of 1933, as it may be amended from time to time.

TENTH: Directors of the corporation shall not be liable to either the corporation or its stockholders for monetary damages for a breach of fiduciary duties unless the breach involves: (1) a director's duty of loyalty to the corporation or its stockholders; (2) acts or omissions not in good faith or which involve intentional misconduct or a knowing violation of law; (3) liability for unlawful payments of dividends or unlawful stock purchases or redemption by the corporation; or (4) a transaction from which the director derived an improper personal benefit.

I. THE UNDERSIGNED, for the purpose of forming a corporation under the laws of the State of Delaware, do make, file and record this certificate, and do certify that the facts herein stated are true; and I have accordingly hereunto set my hand.

DATED AT:_____

_____

REGISTERED AGENTS

SECTION VI

In Delaware there are more than thirty companies that provide "registered agent" services to corporations. There is a list of some ot these companies later in this section. One of the main functions of these companies is to provide a street address for corporations. All corporations formed in Delaware are required to have a mailing address in the state. These service companies that can provide this (and other services) are known as *Registered Agents*.

Annual fees charged by registered agents for providing a Delaware address range from $75 to $250 per year. One of the largest registered agents (who owns several registered agent companies) charges $150 per year. If a lawyer's services are used, there are additional fees of $300—$3000. Registered agents generally charge an additional fee of $60 to $300 for the initial formation of a corporation.

One company, The Company Corporation, charges only $35* per calendar year during the first year for their annual registered agent service. This modest fee is less than that charged by others. This fee increases to $50 for the second year and $68 the third year.

There is *no initial fee* charged for the formation of the corporation. *No* legal fees are necessary since customers of The Company Corporation *complete the forms themselves*. No counseling service is provided or needed if the forms are completed by the person who is forming the corporation.

Service is provided in a highly confidential manner as well as a speedy one. Upon receipt of forms corporation is filed with Secretary of State the *same* day.

Potential savings using The Company Corporation for the initial formation of the corporation is up to $3,000 and up to $250 on an annual basis.

The Company Corporation operates differently than other registered agents. It operates on a volume basis and advertises for its customers on a direct basis. Its fees are substantially less than its competitors. All "middle man" type fees are eliminated.

The Company Corporation will provide services to customers referred by lawyers but does not require this.

All that is required is that a certificate of incorporation and signed Confidential Information form be completed by the customer and sent to The Company Corporation. Certificate is then forwarded to the appropriate places.

No legal advice or counseling is provided by The Company Corporation. Administerial functions only are provided. No review or advice on the form itself can be given. However, if the form is complete (instructions are contained herein) *none is necessary*. If for any reason the certificate of incorporation is not accepted by the Secretary of State in Dover, Delaware it is returned without comment by The Company Corporation with any of the Secretary of State's comments.

In addition to providing a permanent street address in Delaware, The Company Corporation, unlike any other registered agent, provides the following services at *no* cost to its customers:

Initial Service:

1. Act as registered agent and provide a mailing address in Delaware. The Company Corporation provides a mailing address for the purpose of receiving and forwarding all legal documents, not general mail delivery. General mail forwarding can be arranged for an additional fee.

---

* *Prices and fees are subject to change without notice.*

2. Furnish the incorporator. (Certificate of incorporation can be completed but unsigned if desired.)

3. Forward the certificate of incorporation to the Corporation Department in Dover, Delaware for filing.

4. File a copy of the Certificate of Incorporation with the Recorder of Deeds office.

5. Prepare checks for payment of initial recording fees to the State of Delaware.

6. Reserve corporate name and file documents the same day request is received from customer.

7. Order printed stock certificates, corporate seal and forms for minutes and by-laws, if the option is desired by client.

8. Supply the appropriate forms for qualifying the Delaware Corporation in any other state in the United States at the nominal handling charge — $.50 each upon request.

Continuing Services:

9. Process application for federal identification number.

10. Process application for "S" status filings with the IRS.

11. Act as registered agent and provide a mailing address in Delaware.

12. Forward the corporation annual report form to the Secretary of State, Dover, Delaware. Once each year the Secretary of State, Dover, Delaware sends to the Delaware mailing address of every corporation chartered in the State, an annual report form. The Company Corporation forwards this to its customers. It is completed by the customer and sent back to The Company Corporation who then forwards it to the Secretary of State, Dover, Delaware for filing.

13. Referral service to competent Delaware lawyers, if legal counseling or advice is requested on any corporate matter (since the volume of corporate activity is so great in Delaware, many capable lawyers practice there.)

14. Assist in locating facilities for annual meetings if the client wishes to have them and/or hold them in Delaware.

15. Receive legal documents served on the corporation in Delaware, including law suits, and forward these to the business address of the corporation.

16. Publish a periodic newsletter dealing with helpful business ideas that can save money. Also other services that The Company Corporation makes available to its customers are described in the newsletter. Other services through affiliated companies include simplified bookkeeping systems, tax deductible group and individual insurance plans, helpful books and manuals, and patent and trademark searches.

In addition, The Company Corporation will furnish upon request the Delaware fee schedule for filing forms with the state. These include, but are not limited to: increases of number of shares of stock, new classes of stock, amending certificates of incorporation, dissolutions, etc.

A partial list of companies in Delaware that are available to provide services to corporations, including acting as Registered Agent are listed as follows:

No initial fee for filing corporate documents	THE COMPANY CORPORATION
No legal fees necessary	CORPORATION CENTER
Annual Fee: $35.00 first calendar year	725 NORTH MARKET STREET
$50.00 second calendar year	WILMINGTON, DE 19801
$68.00 third year and thereafter	

Initial Fee $60-$300 for filing corporate documents. Legal Fees $300-$3,000 (most of these companies require that clients be referred by lawyer), Annual Fee $75-$250.

American Guaranty & Trust Co.
3801 Kennett Pike
Greenville Center
Wilmington, Delaware 19807

Capital Trust Co. of Delaware
1013 Centre Rd.
Wilmington, Delaware 19805

Colonial Charter Co.
1102 West Street
Wilmington, Delaware 19801

Corporate Systems Inc.
101 North Fairfield Dr.
Dover, Delaware 19801

Corporation Guarantee & Trust Co.
11th Fl., Rodney Square North
11th & Market Streets
Wilmington, Delaware 19801

Corporation Service Co.
1013 Centre Road
Wilmington, Delaware 19805

Corporation Trust Co. (The)
1209 Orange Street
Wilmington, Delaware 19801

Delaware Corporation Organizers,Inc.
1105 North Market Street
Wilmington, Delaware 19899

Delaware Registration Trust Co.
900 Market Street
Wilmington, Delaware 19801

Delaware Registry, LTD.
2316 Baynard Blvd.
Wilmington, Delaware 19802

Incorporating Services, LTD.
410 South State Street
Dover, Delaware 19901

The Incorporators, LTD.
Lancaster Pike & Loveville Rd.
Hockessin, Delaware 19707

Incorporators of Delaware
48 The Green
Dover, Delaware 19901

National Corporate Research, LTD.
15 North Street
Dover, Delaware 19901

Prentice-Hall Corp. System, Inc. (The)
229 South State Street
Dover, Delaware 19901

Registered Agents, LTD.
902 Market Street
Wilmington, Delaware 19899

United Corporate Services, Inc.
229 South State Street
Dover, Delaware 19901

United States Corporation Co.
229 South State Street
Dover, Delaware 19901

THE COMPANY CORPORATION

SECTION VII

Any registered agent listed in this book may assist in filing forms for incorporating and providing other services to corporations. The Company Corporation provides their services in a different manner and at a lower cost than any other company; also, it will assist you in incorporating in the State of Delaware, or any other State of the Union. Should you want to incorporate in any state other than Delaware, call 1-800-533-2665. Ask for a complete set of forms and information for the state that interests you. As a buyer of this book, details will be furnished to you free of charge.

The Company Corporation charges no fee for initial administrative services in filing the certificate of incorporation with the State of Delaware, providing that The Company Corporation is appointed registered agent. Other registered agents charge up to $300 for initial incorporating services, in addition to legal fees charges by a lawyer. The annual fee for engaging The Company Corporation is $35 during the first calendar year and there are no legal fees. The fee gradually increases to $50 the second year and $68 the third year and thereafter. This modest graduating fee is designed to help keep costs as low as possible during the corporation's early formative years.

The only other initial costs to the incorporator are Delaware fees as follows:

$25 covers the cost of filing, receiving and indexing the certificate; $15 is the minimum State Tax (authorized capitalization not exceeding $150,000 or 3,000 no-par shares; 3,000 shares, as previously suggested, results in the lowest fees); $10.00 for a certified copy from the State, and $21.00 for a *one page* certificate, or a total of $71.00. The aggregate amount paid to The Company Corporation at the time the Charter is filed is $106.00. This includes first calendar year fee of $35 for registered agent service.

Most certificates of incorporation run unnecessarily to four or more pages costing $49 or more just to file. The forms in this book, all on one page except non-stock, cost only $9.00 per page plus a $3.00 document recording fee ($21.00 minimum) to file with the Recorder of Deeds. Copy used in the certificates of incorporation contained in this book has been reproduced from forms supplied by the Secretary of State, Dover, Delaware.

Minutes of the first meeting and by-laws may be torn out of this book and used for the new corporation. Stock certificates and corporate seal are available from stationery stores.

As an option to its customers, The Company Corporation makes available the following Corporate Kit:

1. Vinyl covered Record Book to hold corporate records (with extra large holes) size 12" X10" X 1.5", corporate name printed on gold insert.

2. Metal corporate seal imprinted with the corporate name 1-5/8" diameter in a pouch. This can be used on various documents.

3. Twenty (20) lithographed stock certificates of one class of stock all *numbered* and *printed* with *corporate* name and *capitalization*. (If more than one class of stock, you may request price.)

4. Pre-printed minutes and by-laws forms to fit into above book.

5. Tax shelter under Section 1244 of the Internal Revenue Code. Complete set of forms and instructions make it easy to obtain benefits.

The total minimum cost for utilizing The Company Corporation as a registered agent in the State of Delaware is $106.00. With the above optional and useful material, and the additional cost is $44.95, plus $5.00 for U.P.S. delivery, making a total of $155.95. Details and costs for incorporating in other states are available upon request.

By popular request, The Company Corporation will apply for and obtain a Federal Tax I.D. Number and "S" status for the corporation for the nominal fee of $50.00. Allow 30 days for normal I.R.S. turnaround time — which is usually faster than if done by client individually.

Delaware & County Fee	Incorporating Fee—Using The Company Corporation first Year's* Registered Agent Fee	TOTAL
$71.00	$35.00	$106.00
	Optional Corporate Kit	49.95
	($44.95+$5.00 U.P.S.)	
	Apply for "S" Corporation Status (optional)	25.00
	Federal I.D. Number (optional)	25.00
Total Payable to The Company Corporation—including Kit		$205.95**

In rare cases there may be a need for a corporation that differs slightly from the examples in this book, involving more than one class of stock, more shares, etc. The Company Corporation will furnish quotations of what the State of Delaware filing fees are for any type corporation. In no case does The Company Corporation charge more than the $35 annual registered agent fee for filing initial documents as long as they are completed by the customer.

The Company Corporation cannot furnish personal counsel or advise or answer questions to inquiries that involve interpretations or opinions of law.

---

*Annual registered agent fee is payable each **calendar** year. Calendar year begins on January 1st.

**All prices and fees subject to change without notice.

CONFIDENTIAL INFORMATION FORM

(To accompany completed Certificate of Incorporation form)

1. Name of Corporation: _____
   (A) Alternative name if above name is reserved or already being used by another corporation
   _____

2. Nature of business the company will transact: _____
   _____

3. State of Incorporation: _____

4. No. of shares of common stock (up to 3,000 at lowest cost)_____
   (These shares shall be NO PAR VALUE unless otherwise specified.)_____

5. Where is the principal office outside of state of incorporation:_____
   _____

6. Type of corporation _____ open _____ close _____ non stock_____

7. Number of Directors: _____

8. Date and place of regular meeting of stockholders:_____

9. Date and place of regular meeting of Directors: _____

10. Name(s) and address(es) of Director(s): _____
    _____

11. Names of officer(s):(One person may hold all offices):_____
    PRESIDENT _____ VICE PRESIDENT_____
    SECRETARY_____ TREASURER _____

12. Any special instructions: _____

13. Name of Applicant: _____ Daytime Telephone: _____
    No. and Street:_____
    City, State, Zip:_____
    _____

❑ Enclosed is a check payable to The Company Corporation in the amount of_____

❑ Charge my: ❑ Visa   ❑ MasterCard. Card#_____ Exp._____

Signature _____

_____ State Filing Fees (Typically $71.00)	**Where did you purchase this book?**	
_____ Registered Agent Fee (First calendar year service $35.00)	Advertisement in _____	
_____ Corporate Kit ($44.95+$5.00 U.P.S. = $49.95)		
_____ Federal Tax I.D. Number = $25.00	Bookstore _____	
_____ S Status Filing = $25.00		
_____ Deluxe Leather Bound Kit ($149.95)	Direct Mail _____	
_____ Foreign Airmail ($40.00)		
_____ Foreign Qualification	Referred by_____	
_____ Other		
_____ TOTAL	Other_____	

We'll bill you or refund the difference if under or overpaid. NOTE: For rapid service, enclose a certified check, treasurer's check, or money order. Otherwise allow fourteen (14) days for check clearance.

Please send all correspondence relevant to this corporation to:

Name: _____

Address: _____

City: _____ State: _____ Zip: _____

I certify that neither The Company Corporation nor any of its employees or agents have provided me with any personal counsel or advise.

THE COMPANY CORPORATION
725 North Market Street
Wilmington, Delaware 19801

_____
                                    Signature

Would you like to receive offers from carefully screened business mailers who wish to use our mailing list?_____ Yes_____ No

CB02C

CONFIDENTIAL INFORMATION FORM

(To accompany completed Certificate of Incorporation form)

1. Name of Corporation: _____

   (A) Alternative name if above name is reserved or already being used by another corporation

   _____

2. Nature of business the company will transact: _____

   _____

3. State of Incorporation: _____

4. No. of shares of common stock (up to 3,000 at lowest cost)_____

   (These shares shall be NO PAR VALUE unless otherwise specified.)_____

5. Where is the principal office outside of state of incorporation:_____

   _____

6. Type of corporation _____ open _____ close _____ non stock_____

7. Number of Directors: _____

8. Date and place of regular meeting of stockholders:_____

9. Date and place of regular meeting of Directors: _____

10. Name(s) and address(es) of Director(s): _____

    _____

11. Names of officer(s):(One person may hold all offices):_____

    PRESIDENT _____ VICE PRESIDENT_____

    SECRETARY_____ TREASURER _____

12. Any special instructions: _____

13. Name of Applicant: _____ Daytime Telephone: _____

    No. and Street:_____

    City, State, Zip:_____

    _____

❑ Enclosed is a check payable to The Company Corporation in the amount of_____

❑ Charge my: ❑ Visa   ❑ MasterCard. Card# _____ Exp._____

Signature _____

_____ State Filing Fees (Typically $71.00)	Where did you purchase this book?
_____ Registered Agent Fee (First calendar year service $35.00)	Advertisement in _____
_____ Corporate Kit ($44.95+$5.00 U.P.S. = $49.95)	
_____ Federal Tax I.D. Number = $25.00	Bookstore _____
_____ S Status Filing = $25.00	
_____ Deluxe Leather Bound Kit ($149.95)	Direct Mail _____
_____ Foreign Airmail ($40.00)	
_____ Foreign Qualification	Referred by_____
_____ Other	
_____ TOTAL	Other_____

We'll bill you or refund the difference if under or overpaid. NOTE: For rapid service, enclose a certified check, treasurer's check, or money order. Otherwise allow fourteen (14) days for check clearance.

Please send all correspondence relevant to this corporation to:

Name: _____

Address: _____

City: _____ State: _____ Zip: _____

I certify that neither The Company Corporation nor any of its employees or agents have provided me with any personal counsel or advise.

THE COMPANY CORPORATION

725 North Market Street

Wilmington, Delaware 19801

_____
                                    Signature

Would you like to receive offers from carefully screened business mailers who wish to use our mailing list?_____ Yes_____ No

CB02C

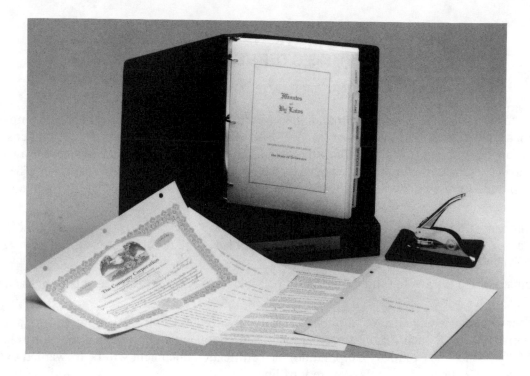

The Company Corporation will provide a complete "kit" which includes:

1. **Handsome Gold Stamping on Black Vinyl Binder and Slip Case** to protect records. Your corporate name will be printed on a gold insert for the spine of the binder.

2. **Corporate Seal**—fits in your pocket, or can be kept in the pouch inside the binder. The seal is often required for completion of legal documents, such as: leases and purchase agreements. Your corporate name and year of incorporation are permanently etched into dies which create a raised impression on any paper. (Seal sold separately is $20.00 for up to 45 characters.)

3. **Minutes and By-laws** printed on three-hole paper for easy permanent record. Complete forms are included for any Delaware corporation, along with instructions.

4. **20 Lithographed Stock Certificates** printed with your corporate name on each certificate. Rich background design. Printing also includes number of shares authorized by corporation. (Additional stock certificates can be purchased. Minimum purchase is 20 @ $18.50 total; 21-100 @ $.65 each; over 100 @ $.25 each.)

5. **Celluloid Tab Index Separators** make it easy to turn to any section in the binder.

6. **Stock Transfer Ledger** to keep an accurate and complete record of any stock sold in your corporation.

7. **Extra blank** pages for any business purpose. (Additional blanks at $3 per 100.)

Overall size is 12" x 10" x 1 1/2"—A beautiful addition to any library or desk. All the above is $49.95*, delivered anywhere in the world.

A deluxe genuine leather Binder and Corporate Kit with your corporate name stamped in gold and containing all of the above (with the exception of the optional membership certificates) is available at $149.95*.

*Price includes $5.00 for U.P.S. delivery.

EXISTING CORPORATIONS THAT WISH TO CHANGE REGISTERED AGENTS

SECTION VII—A

In order for an existing *Delaware* corporation to obtain the advantages offered by The Company Corporation, a simple form is all that is necessary. If a person wishes to change agents the total cost to that corporation the first year is $61.00. This is the actual filing cost that is paid to the State of Delaware. This is less than existing corporations are charged by their present Registered Agent each year. The fee is $40.00 to file the form with the Secretary of State and $21.00 to the Recorder of Deeds for a total of $61.00.

The Company Corporation will provide its registered agent services at no cost during the first calendar year to existing corporations. Thereafter, its annual fee is $68.00. This is an annual savings of at least $25.00 and up to $200.00.

A specimen of the Delaware form that makes it possible to change registered agents is on the next page.

If a reader wishes to avail himself of this low cost service, write The Company Corporation for a copy of this form in duplicate. By mailing this form and completed Confidential Information form with a check for $61.00 (payable to The Company Corporation) the certification document will be forwarded to the Secretary of State's office in Dover, Delaware for filing.

If the corporation has its present office in Kent or Sussex County, prepare an additional copy of the form and add $5.50 to the amount, making a total of $66.50.

CERTIFICATE OF CHANGE OF LOCATION OF REGISTERED
OFFICE AND REGISTERED AGENT
OF

_____

The board of directors of the_____

a corporation of Delaware, on this _____day of _____

A.D. 19____ do hereby resolve and order that the location of the registered office of this corporation

within this State be, and the same hereby is _____ , in

the City of _____ , in the County of _____ .

    The name of the registered agent therein and in charge thereof upon whom process against this

corporation may be served is _____ .

    The_____ , a corporation of Delaware, doth hereby cer-

tify that the foregoing is a true copy of a resolution adopted by the board of directors at a meeting held

as herein stated.

    IN WITNESS WHEREOF, said corporation has caused this certificate to be signed by its

President and Attested by its Secretary, and its corporate seal to be hereto affixed, the _____ day

of _____ A.D. 19 _____ .

By _____

(SEAL)   PRESIDENT

ATTEST:

_____

SECRETARY

STATE FEE FOR QUALIFYING DELAWARE CORPORATIONS IN OTHER STATES

SECTION VIII

A Delaware corporation that has all or most of its activities in another state is supposed to register the corporation in that state. Many Delaware corporations fail to register in other states. The hazard in not qualifying is usually a small fine and payment of a registration fee. Also, the unqualified Delaware corporation may not be able to use the courts of another state. Anyone can write to the Secretary of State in any State to determine its policy on "foreign" corporations who have not registered within that state.

In the following pages are the fees and taxes charged by each state for "qualifying" a Delaware corporation in another state as a "Foreign" corporation. The list of fees is broken down into initial and continuing fees, i.e., if a Minnesota resident has his business in Minnesota and forms a Delaware corporation, he is supposed to pay the home state a fee for "qualifying" a "foreign" corporation. The qualification procedure for "foreign" corporations is simple and can be accomplished at any time. A Delaware registered agent can file a copy of the certificate of incorporation with any particular state or states anytime during the life of the corporation. The Company Corporation provides this service to its customers at a processing cost of $25.00.

There are businesses that legally circumvent paying fees to home state by establishing that they are "doing business" in Delaware and not in another state.

Examples would include corporations that receive and ship materials from Delaware, mail order businesses who use a Delaware office, corporations that own property in Delaware and franchise or licensing companies who transact all contracts and orders in Delaware.

As to out of state residents who incorporate in Delaware, the Secretary of State's office in Dover, Delaware does not notify any other state as to who the new Delaware corporation owners or shareholders are or in what state they have a business office.

On the following pages there are fees for all states outlined. Initial filing fees, pages 42-45, minimum annual fees pages 47-49. The fees charged by the various states are, of course, subject to change. If an additional certified copy of a Delaware Certificate of Incorporation is required by another state, Delaware's fee is $11.00 for a one page certificate. A certificate of good standing, required by some states, is $10.00.

QUALIFICATION OF A DELAWARE CORPORATION
(One Time Fee)

SECTION IX

Each state's Corporation Department assesses fees to all corporations "foreign" to that state:

STATE

ALABAMA*

Filing certified copy of Articles of Incorporation	$110.00
Initial Tax (minimum)	25.00
Annual Franchise Tax	25.00
Fee for annual Permit (minimum)	5.00
Filing Designation of Agent	10.00
Total Minimum Fee	$175.00

ALASKA**

Initial fee based on authorized capital stock (minimum)	$153.00
Filing appointment of Commissioner of Commerce as agent	12.00
Annual Corporation Tax	200.00
Total Minimum Fee	$365.00

ARIZONA***

Filing Application	$150.00
Total Minimum Fee	$150.00

ARKANSAS*

Filing Application	$350.00
Total Minimum Fee	$350.00

CALIFORNIA**

Filing Statement	$350.00
Franchise Tax (minimum)	800.00
Total Minimum Fee	$1150.00

COLORADO**

Filing application for, and issuing Certificate of Authority	$50.00
Total Minimum Fee	$50.00

CONNECTICUT**

Initial license fee	$315.00
Filing application for Certificate of Authority	180.00
Total Minimum Fee	$495.00

DISTRICT OF COLUMBIA*

Filing and indexing application	$22.00
Total Minimum Fee	$22.00

STATE

FLORIDA**

Tax on capital employed or to be employed (minimum)	$30.00
Filing Designation of Agent	3.00
Issuing permit to do business	7.00
Total Minimum Fee	$40.00

GEORGIA**

Filing application and issuing Certificate of Authority	$170.00
Total Minimum Fee	$170.00

HAWAII**

Qualification Fee	$50.00
Annual License Fee (prorated from 1st of month in which business is begun to following July 1st)	100.00
Total Minimum Fee	$150.00

IDAHO**

Filing articles of incorporation (minimum)	$24.00
Filing and recording Designation	4.00
Fees for certifying qualification forms (minimum, approx.)	3.00
Issuing certificate of qualification	4.00
Annual License Tax (minimum, but prorated)	20.00
To County Recorder	3.00
Total Minimum Fee	$60.00

ILLINOIS*

Filing Application	$75.00
Initial License Fee (minimum)	.50
Franchise Tax (minimum, but prorated)	25.00
Total Minimum Fee	$100.50

INDIANA**

Filing Application (minimum)	$90.00
Total Minimum Fee	$90.00

STATE

IOWA**
Filing Application	$100.00
Total Minimum Fee	$100.00

KANSAS**
Application Fee	$75.00
Capitalization fee (minimum)	10.00
Filing and recording fee to Secretary of State	3.00
Recording Fee to Register of Deeds	7.00
Total Minimum Fee	$95.00

KENTUCKY*
Filing certified copy of Articles of Incorporation	$80.00
Recording certified copy of Articles of Incorporation	10.00
Total Minimum Fee	$90.00

LOUISIANA**
Filing Application	$100.00
Total Minimum Fee	$100.00

MAINE**
Filing Power of Attorney Filing Foreign Corporation Certificate	$100.00
Total Minimum Fee	$100.00

MARYLAND**
Filing certified copy of charter Certificate of Compliance	$50.00
Total Minimum Fee	$50.00

MASSACHUSETTS**
Filing charter and by-laws	$300.00
Total Minimum Fee	$300.00

MICHIGAN**
Franchise Fee (minimum)	$50.00
For filing and examining certified copy of charter	10.00
Total Minimum Fee	$60.00

MINNESOTA*
Initial License Fee	$161.00
Filing Application for and issuing Certificate of Authority	19.00
Recording Fee	5.00
Total Minimum Fee	$185.00

STATE

MISSISSIPPI*
Filing Application for Certificate of Authority (minimum)	$525.00
Total Minimum Fee	$525.00

MISSOURI**
On proportion of capital represented (minimum)	$60.00
Total Minimum Fee	$60.00

MONTANA***
Filing Application for Certificate of Authority and issuing Certificate of Authority	$20.00
License Fee	50.00
Total Minimum Fee	$70.00

NEBRASKA**
Filing Application for Certificate of Authority	$113.00
Issuing Certificate of Authority	1.00
Recording Application and Certificate of Authority	2.00
Total Minimum Fee	$116.00

NEVADA**
Filing certificate of incorporation (minimum)	
Certifying copy of charter	
Filing List of Officers and Directors	
Filing copy of certificate of incorporation with county Clerk	$135.00
Total Minimum Fee	$135.00

NEW HAMPSHIRE**
Registration Fee	$275.00
Total Minimum Fee	$275.00

NEW JERSEY**
Filing Application for Certificate of Authority	$100.00
Total Minimum Fee	$100.00

NEW MEXICO**
Filing fee based on authorized capital stock (minimum)	$100.00
Total Minimum Fee	$100.00

STATE

NEW YORK**
Certificate of Authority	$200.00
Total Minimum Fee	$200.00

NORTH CAROLINA*
Fee on authorized capital stock (minimum)	$80.00
Filing Fee	10.00
Total Minimum Fee	$90.00

NORTH DAKOTA**
Initial License Fee	$75.00
Filing Application for Certificate of Authority	40.00
Consent of Registered Agent	$10.00
Total Minimum Fee	$125.00

OHIO**
Filing Fee	$75.00
Total Minimum Fee	$75.00

OKLAHOMA**
Initial Fee (on capital invested) (minimum)	
Filing Articles of Domestication and issuing Certificate of Domestication	$340.00
Total Minimum Fee	$340.00

OREGON**
Filing Application for Certificate of authority	$220.00
Annual License Fee	220.00
Total Minimum Fee	$440.00

PENNSYLVANIA**
Filing Application for Certificate of Authority	$150.00
Total Minimum Fee	$150.00

PUERTO RICO**
Filing certified Copy of Charter	$190.00
Total Minimum Fee	$190.00

RHODE ISLAND*
Filing Fee	$65.00
Total Minimum Fee	$65.00

STATE

SOUTH CAROLINA**
Filing Application for Certificate of Authority	$85.00
Additional tax on Capital (minimum)	40.00
First Report	10.00
Total Minimum Fee	$135.00

SOUTH DAKOTA*
Filing Application for Certificate of Authority (minimum)	$40.00
Total Minimum Fee	$40.00

TENNESSEE**
Filing Application for Certificate of Authority	$ 300.00
Total Minimum Fee	$300.00

TEXAS***
Deposit to controller of Public Account	$ 500.00
Franchise Tax	100.00
Filing Application for Certificate of Authority	500.00
Total Minimum Fee	$1100.00

UTAH**
Filing Application for and issuing Certificate of Authority	$25.00
License fee (minimum)	25.00
Total Minimum Fee	$50.00

VERMONT*
For issuing Certificate of Authority	$100.00
Total Minimum Fee	$100.00

VIRGINIA*
Par Value Shares	
Fee on authorized capital stock ($50,000 or less $30; 60 cents per $1,000 up to $1,000,000 etc.)	$70.00
No Par Value Shares	
Assessed at $100/share	
Filing Application for Certificate of Authority	5.00
Total Minimum Fee	$75.00

STATE

WASHINGTON**

Filing Application	$175.00
Total Minimum Fee	$175.00

WEST VIRGINIA **(2) *(2)

Issuing Certificate of Authority	$10.00
Annual License Tax (prorated)	250.00
Tax on Land (5 cents per acre in excess of 10,000 acre)	
Fee to State Auditor for acting as resident attorney (prorated)	10.00
Recording charter and Certificate of Authority (est. minimum)	$5.00
Total Minimum Fee	$275.00

STATE

WISCONSIN*

Filing application for Certificate of Authority (minimum) (Based on capital employed or to be employed)	$75.00
Total Minimum Fee	$75.00

WYOMING*

Filing application for and issuing Certificate of Authority	$51.00
In addition there is tax of $1.00 per $1,000 in assets	
Total Minimum Fee	$51.00

---

* Certified copy of Certificate of Incorporation Required

** Certificate of Good Standing Required

*** A $500 deposit by separate cashier's check is payable to Comptroller of Public Accounts.

Both documents can be obtained directly through a registered agent.

TOTAL APPROXIMATE QUALIFICATION FEES
FOR ALL 50 STATES $11,079.50

Either a certified copy of the Certificate of Incorporation (also called Articles of Incorporation) or certificates of good standing are required in most states. Additional copies of the validated Certificate of Incorporation can be obtained from the Secretary of State's office in Dover, Delaware. Cost is $11.00 for certified copy and $10.00 for certificate of good standing.

(The Company Corporation will supply you with qualification forms for any State at $.50 each for postage and handling.)

As legislation can and does change rapidly, it is advisable to check with the individual State regarding current fee schedules and regulations.

MINIMUM ANNUAL FEE PAYABLE TO
CORPORATION DEPARTMENT
FOR FOREIGN AND DOMESTIC CORPORATIONS

SECTION IX—A

STATE	TAX	FOREIGN	DOMESTIC
Ala.	Annual Permit	$5.	$10.
	Franchise Tax	$25.	$50.
Alaska	Biennial Corporation Tax	$200.	$200.
	Business License Tax	$25.	$25.
Ariz.	Annual Report	$30.	$30.
Ark.	Franchise Tax	$17.	$7.
Calif.	Franchise (Income)Tax	$200.	$200.
	Annual Report	—	$5.
Colo.	Biennial Report	$70.	$18.
Conn.	Income (Fran.) Tax	$100.	$100.
	License Fee	$150.	(Not Subject)
	Biennial Report	$70.	$70.
Del.	Franchise Tax	(Not Subject)	$30.
	Annual Report	$40.	$10.
D.C.	Franchise (Income)Tax	$100.	$100.
	Annual Report	$50.	$25.
Fla.	Annual Report	$20.	$20.
Ga.	Annual License Tax	$10.	$10.
	Annual Report Fee	$10.	$10.
Hawaii	Annual License Fee	$100.	(Not Subject)
	Annual Corp. Exhibit	$10.	$10.
Ida.	Annual License Tax	$20.	$20.
Ill.	Franchise Tax	$25.	$25.
	Annual Report	$15.	$15.
Ind.	Annual Report	$15.	$15.
Iowa	Annual License Fee	$15.	$15.

STATE	TAX	FOREIGN	DOMESTIC
Kan.	Franchise Tax	$20.	$20.
Ky.	Annual License Fee	$30.	$30.
	Statement of Existence	$4.	(Not Subject)
	Annual Verification Rpt.	$5.	$5.
	Annual Name Renewal Fee.	$12.	(Not Subject)
LA.	Franchise Tax	$10.	$10.
	Filing Annual Report	$5.	$5.
Me.	Filing fee for Annual Report	$30.	$30.
Md.	Filing Fee Annual Rpt.	(Not Subject)	$40.
	Personal Property Ret.	$40.	(No Fee)
Mass.	Corporation Excise Tax	$200.	$200.
	Cert. of Condition Annual Report	$70.	$70.
Mich.	Annual Report	$15.	$15.
Minn.	Corporate License Fee	$30.	$10.
	Annual Report	$20.	(Not Subject)
Miss.	Franchise Tax	$25.	$25.
	Annual Report	$10.	$10.
Mo.	Franchise Tax	$25.	$25.
	Registration Statement	$10.	$10.
Mont.	License Tax	$50.	$50.
	Annual Report	$10.	$10.
Neb.	Corporation "Occupation" Tax	$13.	$13.
Nev.	List of Officers, Directors and Agent	$30.	$30.
N.H.	Franchise Tax	$150.	$60.
	Annual Report	$60.	$60.
N.J.	Net Worth Tax	$50.	$25.
	Annual Report	$15.	$15.
N.M.	Franchise Tax	$15.	$15.
	Annual Report	$10.	$20.
N.Y.	Franchise (Income)Tax	$250.	$250.
	Annual Maintenance Fee	$200.	(Not Subject)
N.C.	Franchise Tax	$10.	$10.
N.D.	Annual Filing Fee	$20.	$10.

STATE	TAX	FOREIGN	DOMESTIC
Ohio	Franchise Tax	$50.	$50.
Okla.	Franchise Tax	$10.	$10.
	Secretary of State	$40.	—
	Annual Affidavit	$3.	—
Ore.	License Fee	$220.	$15.
Penna.	Capital Stock Tax	$150.	$75.
Puerto Rico	Annual Report	$100.	$100.
	License Fee	$25.	—
R.I.	Annual Franchise Tax	(Not Subject)	$100.
	Annual Report	$15.	$15.
S.C.	License Tax	$15.	$15.
S.D.	Annual Report	$10.	$10.
Tenn.	Franchise Tax	$10.	$10.
	Annual Report	$10.	$10.
Texas	Franchise Tax	$68.	$68.
Utah	Franchise (Income)Tax	$100.	$100.
	Annual Report	$5.	$5.
Vt.	Corporate Income Tax	$75.	$75.
	Annual Report	$100.	—
Va.	Franchise Tax	—	$20.
	Registration Fee	$25.	$25.
	Annual Report	$5.	$5.
Wash.	License Fee	$50.	$50.
	Annual Report	$5.	$5.
W.Va.	License Tax	$250.	$20.
	Fee to Secretary of State		
	Attorney-in-fact	$10.	$10.
Wisc.	Annual Report	$28.	$13
Wyo.	License Tax	$10.	$10.

COMMON, PREFERRED, VOTING AND NON-VOTING STOCK

SECTION X

A corporation may issue common or preferred stock with or without par value.

Usually preferred stockholders have priority rights over common stockholders in the event a corporation is liquidated or dissolved. Also, preferred stock usually does not have voting privileges.

Stock in a corporation may also have conditions imposed upon it which permit stockholders either to have or not to have voting privileges. Voting or non-voting stock is usually designated by class, such as class A-voting stock, class B-non-voting stock.

Capital stock can also be issued with a stated value paid for either in cash or by providing services to the corporation. However, under Delaware Corporate Law, no capital is required by a Delaware corporation.

A Delaware corporation may file simple forms with the Secretary of State to add provisions for any of the above types of stock at any time after the corporation is formed.

The forms in this book are directed to a corporation with one class of stock. No par common stock shares (with voting privileges) of up to 3,000 shares are used in the specimen forms. The filing fees both initial and continuing are lowest with this type of format. Also, this kind of approach to the type of stock is simple and services the needs of most small and medium sized corporations.

On an annual basis, franchise tax is based on the number of authorized shares of stock, irrespective of par value. It's an unnecessary expense to authorize more shares of stock than those necessary to meet the needs of the corporation. On 3,000 shares the annual tax is only $30.00. Examples of fees for more shares are as follows: on i.e. 100,000 shares it is $385.00 and on 1,000,000 shares it is $3,850.00

If, however, it is desirable to issue other classes of stock initially, this can be easily accomplished by adding language to this effect on the certificate of incorporation, before it is filed with the state.

A registered agent can quote what the state filing fees are for the various types of stock or they may be obtained directly from the Secretary of State, Dover, Delaware.

"NO-PAR" VS. "PAR VALUE" STOCK

SECTION XI

Prior to the 1940's, it was customary for most corporations to issue "par value" stock. This meant that each share had a stated value on its face, such as $3.00, which supposedly represented the amount contributed by the shareholder. However, the value of a share of stock can fluctuate greatly, depending on the overall worth of the corporation, so that the "par value" of the stock becomes misleading and unimportant.

Another type of stock has therefore become increasingly more popular. It is called "no-par value" stock. Under this method, a certificate of stock has no stated value, but merely indicates the number of shares of "no-par value". The actual value would depend on what an investor is willing to pay, and this judgment is based on a number of factors. These factors include the assets owned by the corporation and on assessment by the investors as to the corporation's potential profitability.

In addition, the initial filing fee and annual fees to the State of Delaware are lowest when the corporation issues 3,000 shares or less than $300,000 contributed capital. The minimum filing fee is only $15. The type of stock used as examples in this book is "no-par". "No-par value" stock can be converted to "par value" stock by a corporation merely by filing a simple form with the State of Delaware. This can be forwarded to the Secretary of State by a registered agent including The Company Corporation at a nominal filing fee. On the whole, it's usually simpler and less costly to form a Delaware corporation and qualify it to do business in any state with its shares being no par. At the time of printing there is one exception to our knowledge — Virginia. For Virginia, forming Delaware corporations and qualifying to do business in a home state, it is less costly to originally file the corporation with par value stock.

If a corporation becomes successful and authorizes more shares, as well as acquires substantial assets, there can be substantial annual savings in Delaware Corporate Franchise Taxes by converting the no-par value stock to par value stock.

To raise capital, a corporation can also issue bonds which are usually an interest bearing instrument. A bond is a form of debt financing many corporations prefer over the sale of stock.

In business judgments involving decisions of this type, many times it is desirable to consider ideas of authors, accountants, life insurance advisors, trust officers, lawyers, and other sources of information.

ONLY ONE OFFICER

SECTION XII

The Delaware corporation need only have one person that holds all the company offices. This same individual may act as the incorporator. Likewise, the same person can be the entire board of directors. One officer is the legal minimum.

On the other hand, one can have as many directors, officers or vice presidents as desired. Many corporations find it helpful to invite to its board of directors capable people who may often make substantial contributions in building a successful corporation.

Under a new amendment to Delaware Corporate Law, there is substantially greater flexibility than ever before in many areas, including cutting the number of officers from a minimum of three down to one. Previously, a corporation had to have at least three officers — president, secretary and treasurer. The only requirement now is to have one officer. This enables the corporation to have available a person to sign stock certificates and keep minutes of stockholder and director's meetings when appropriate.

THE CORPORATE NAME

SECTION XIII

The name picked for the new corporation when it is submitted to Delaware will be recorded as long as it is in proper form and as long as no one else is using the same name or one that is too similar, prior to the application of the new corporation. *The name must contain the word association, corporation, club, foundation, fund, company, incorporated, institute, society, union, syndicate, or limited, or one of the abbreviations Co., Corp., Inc., or Ltd.*

Delaware will permit words like the ones above in abbreviated form, provided that are written in Roman characters or letters. Corporate names must be distinguishable on the records of the state from the names of other corporations formed under the laws of Delaware.

A service is provided by the state whereby a corporate name can be reserved for a period of thirty (30) days at no charge. Any person can write the state directly to avail himself of this service. However, it is not necessary that this be done. Registered agents provide this service, usually at low cost.

There are certain property rights under the law which accrue to the original owners of a business name or to a corporation that originates a name. These businesses may legally prevent a new firm from using a name that is the same or similar to theirs. If it is planned that the corporation will qualify as a foreign corporation (see Section VIII) in any state, the corporate name is registered in that state by the act of such a filing. Sometimes a name is available in Delaware but not in another state in which the corporation wishes to qualify. When this occurs the corporate name can easily be changed. Filing cost is $50.00 and $21.00 to Recorder of Deeds for a total of $71.00. Form is available from Secretary of State, Dover, Delaware. Your registered agent can also assist you at a modest cost.

POTENTIAL PROBLEMS WITH A CORPORATION'S NAME

The effect of a name change varies. Sometimes it just involves new stationery with notification to people with whom the corporation does business. In other cases substantial cost be incurred, i.e., when a large inventory of packaged goods bear the name. Some businesses use a name change to marketing advantage. Many corporations who have been well established choose to change their name to create a different "image" or to reflect a different line of products or services than existed when the corporation was formed. It is wise to check the yellow pages of the telephone directory when first planning to use a name to see if similar ones exist.

To reduce the possibility of a name change one can contact the Corporation Department in any state to determine if the name is available in advance of filing the form.

When it is known that an existing business uses a certain name, it is prudent not to select a name that is similar to that regardless of where that company is located. Theoretically, a name can be registered in all fifty states to avoid the possibility of a later name change. However, owners of corporations seldom go to this extent. Also an unincorporated business somewhere in the U.S. may be using the same name that the corporation might use and the right to the name could be challenged at some future time. Therefore, unless one were to search every business name in the nation there is always the possibility of a name change at some time during the life of a corporation.

OPERATING ANONYMOUSLY IF DESIRED

SECTION XIV

Many people who are owner(s) of Delaware corporations prefer to remain as anonymous as possible.

In Delaware, a corporation need not disclose who its stockholders are to the Secretary of State. If a person does not wish to disclose who the officer(s) and/or director(s) are, there are three ways this can be accomplished.

The first method is by having an acquaintance, friend or relative of the founder(s) hold all the company offices. This person does not have to be a stockholder in the corporation. (This person, however, should be advised that he could be liable in the event of tax delinquency or for any illegal action by the founder.)

The second way is to obtain and register a legal fictitious name (many authors use this approach commonly called a "pen" name.) A fictitious name can be registered in a Prothonotary's office in Delaware for $15.00. Other states have a similar procedure. Then this name can be used for corporate purposes and to sign checks, etc. Registering a fictitious name can be accomplished where you reside at the Recorder of Deeds or Prothonotary's office (or its equivalent, county clerk, etc.) or in Delaware.

The third method is by the corporation not filing the annual report to the Secretary of State's office. This report is a simple form that is completed once each year. It basically indicates who the corporation's officers are, how many shares of stock have been authorized, and other data on the corporation's assets. It lists officer(s), director(s), and number of shares. The state imposes a $50.00 annual fine to corporations who do not file this report. Many Delaware corporations have in the past years elected to pay this annual fine rather than file the report, although the state frowns on this practice.

The first and second methods are simpler and less costly, and therefore, are recommended over the third for persons who wish to operate the corporation anonymously.

DEDUCTION OF CORPORATE STOCK LOSS FROM PERSONAL INCOME

SECTION XV

A valuable tax law exists that is beneficial to shareholders of a corporation.

Internal Revenue Code, Section 1244, enables a shareholder to deduct certain losses in investment of stock as ordinary income losses. Experienced tax lawyers sometimes advise their clients of the existence of this tax law.

Under Section 1244 and subject to its conditions, should a shareholder in a corporation (shareholder can be any individual, but not a corporation, estate or trust) incur any kind of loss through sale of his stock at a loss or if the stock becomes worthless, this section enables a deduction of the loss up to $50,000 a year ($100,000 on a joint return) from personal income. Normally a loss on a stock investment is subject to special "capital loss limitations" under the Internal Revenue Code. Shareholders have nothing to lose, since there are no disadvantages of qualifying the corporation under this tax provision if the corporation is eligible, as most small ones are. The potential tax benefits are well worth it. Also, more investors are potentially attracted toward the purchase of stock in the corporation when the person is made aware of this provision. Of course, a person should always be cautious in how and to whom stock in a corporation is offered so that the Federal Securities regulations under the Securities Act of 1933 are not violated.

What must be done is to merely arrange to have this legal principle put into effect upon the formation of the corporation by completing simple forms. Nothing has to filed with the Internal Revenue Service. A copy of the Internal Revenue Section 1244 is on the following page. One registered agent service company, The Company Corporation, provides standard forms to all clients as a standard part of their service.(See Section VII)

NOTE: Every "Sub-Chapter S" corporation (See Section XVI) should qualify under Section 1244. "Sub-Chapter S" and Section 1244 complement each other in the tax advantages they provide. Operating losses of a "Sub-Chapter S" corporation may be passed on to the stockholders currently; a loss in value in the assets of Section 1244 corporation can be taken as an "ordinary loss" on the sale and exchange of stock.

SECTION 1244. LOSSES ON SMALL BUSINESS STOCK.

(a) GENERAL RULE.—In the case of an individual, a loss on section 1244 stock issued to such individual or to a partnership which would (but for this section) be treated as a loss from the sale or exchange of a capital asset shall, to the extent provided in this section, be treated as an ordinary loss.

(b) MAXIMUM AMOUNT FOR ANY TAXABLE YEAR.—For any taxable year the aggregate amount treated by the taxpayers by reason of this section as an ordinary loss shall not exceed—

(1) $50,000 or

(2) $100,000 in the case of a husband and wife filing a joint return for such year under section 6013.

(c) SECTION 1244 STOCK DEFINED.—

(1) IN GENERAL.— For purposes of this section, the term "section 1244 stock" means common stock in a domestic corporation if—

(A) at the time such stock is issued, such corporation was a small business corporation,

(B) such stock was issued by such corporation for money or other property (other than stock and securities), and

(C) such corporation, during the period of its 5 most recent taxable years ending before the date and loss on such stock was sustained, derived more than 50 percent of its aggregate gross receipts from sources other than royalties, rents, dividends, interests, annuities, and sales or exchanges of stocks or securities.

(2) RULES FOR APPLICATION OF PARAGRAPH (1)(C).—

(A) Period taken into account with respect to new corporations.—For purposes of paragraph (1)(C), if the corporation has not been in existence for 5 taxable years ending before the date the loss on the stock was sustained, there shall be substituted for such 5-year period—

(i) the period of the corporation's taxable years ending before such date, or

(ii) if the corporation has not been in existence for 1 taxable year ending before such date, the period such corporation has been in existence before such date.

(B) Gross receipts from sales of securities.—For purposes of paragraph (1)(C), gross receipts from the sales or exchanges of stock or securities shall be taken into account only to the extent of gains therefrom.

(C) Nonapplication where deductions exceed gross income.—Paragraph (1)(C) shall not apply with respect to any corporation if, for the period taken into account for purposes of paragraph (1)(C), the amount of the deductions allowed by this chapter (other than by sections 172, 243, 244, and 245) exceeds the amount of gross income.

(3) SMALL BUSINESS CORPORATION DEFINED.—

(A) In general.—For purposes of this section, a corporation shall be treated as a small business corporation if the aggregate amount of money and other property received by the corporation for stock, as a contribution to capital, and as paid-in surplus, does not exceed $1,000,000. The determination under the preceding sentence shall be made as of the time of the issuance of the stock in question but shall include amounts received for such stock and for all stock theretofore issued.

(B) Amount taken into account with respect to property.—For purposes of subparagraph (A), the amount taken into account with respect to any property other than money shall be the amount equal to the adjusted basis to the corporation of such property for determining gain, reduced by any liability to which the property was subject or which was assumed by the corporation. The determination under the preceding sentence shall be made as of the time the property was received by the corporation.

(d) SPECIAL RULES.—

(1) LIMITATIONS ON AMOUNT OF ORDINARY LOSS.—

(A) Contributions of property having basis in excess of value.—If—

(i) section 1244 stock was issued in exchange for property.

(ii) the basis of such stock in the hands of the taxpayer is determined by reference to the basis in his hands of such property, and

(iii) the adjusted basis (for determining loss) of such property immediately before the exchange exceeded its fair market value at such time, then in computing the amount of the loss on such stock for purposes of this section the basis of such stock shall be reduced by an amount equal to the excess described in clause (iii).

(B) Increases in basis.—In computing the amount of the loss on stock for purposes of this section, any increase in the basis of such stock (through contributions to the capital of the corporation, or otherwise) shall be treated as allocable to stock which is not section 1244 stock.

(2) RECAPITALIZATION, CHANGES IN NAME, ETC.—To the extent provided in regulations prescribed by the Secretary, common stock in a corporation, the basis of which (in the hands of a taxpayer) is determined in whole or in part by reference to the basis in his hands of stock in such corporation which meets the requirements of sub-section (c)(1) (other than subparagraph (C) thereof), or which is received in a reorganization described in section 368(a)(1)(F) in exchange for stock which meets such requirements, shall be treated as meeting such requirements. For purposes of paragraphs (1)(C) and (3)(A) of subsection (c), a successor corporation in a reorganization described in section 368(a)(1)(F) shall be treated as the same corporation as its predecessor.

(3) RELATIONSHIP TO NET OPERATING LOSS DEDUCTION.—For purposes of section 172 (relating to the net operating loss deduction), any amount of loss treated by reason of this section as an ordinary loss shall be treated as attributable to a trade or business of the taxpayer.

(4) INDIVIDUAL DEFINED.—For purposes of this section, the term individual does not include a trust or estate.

(e) REGULATIONS.—The Secretary shall prescribe such regulations as may be necessary to carry out the purposes of this section.

"S" CORPORATION —
BENEFITS OF CORPORATIONS TAXED AS A
PROPRIETORSHIP OR PARTNERSHIP

SECTION XVI

Under the new tax reform, forming an "S" Corporation makes possible the best of all worlds — the benefits of incorporation with the new low individual rates (see page before Suggested Readings).

A corporation normally pays tax on its profits at corporate rates (page 5). Tax is again owed — this time by stockholders — when dividends are paid.

Fortunately, this double taxation can easily be completely eliminated by bringing your corporation under the "S" corporation status. As an "S" corporation, earnings are taxed only once. Rather than being taxed to the corporation, profits are included in your personal return and taxed at your individual rates.

If an "S" corporation has a loss for the year, the loss is passed directly out to your own tax return, reducing your personal tax bill. Losses of a regular "C" corporation must be retained in the business for possible later offset against corporate earnings. Stockholders receive no immediate benefit.

"S" corporation tax breaks are available without loss of limited liability, easy transferability of stock, and other advantages available only to a corporation.

*A person can call any Internal Revenue office and obtain Form 2553. This is a one page form which permits tax filing as an "S" corporation. Corporations eligible to elect this tax status must meet five simple requirements. The following is a quotation from Form 2553; "Corporations eligible to elect.— The election may be made only if the corporation is a domestic corporation which meets all five of the following requirements:

1. It has no more than thirty-five shareholders; however, if stock is held by husband and wife as joint tenants, tenants by the entirety, or tenants in common, or is community property (or the income from which is community income), it shall be treated as owned by one shareholder.

2. It has only individuals, estates or certain trusts as shareholders.

3. It has no shareholder who is a non-resident alien.

4. If has only one class of stock.

5. It is not a member of an affiliated group of corporations as defined in Section 1504 of the Code.

A complete set of forms for filing for "S" corporation status is included in this chapter or can be obtained from any IRS office. These forms can be completed without professional help. However, any good accountant can assist in completing this form if desired. The Company Corporation can provide assistance for a fee of $25.00.

---

* *The Company Corporation can obtain S status for your corporation for the nominal fee of $25.00*

** *For a complete S Corporation Handbook, see information and order form on page preceding Section XXIII.*

Department of the Treasury
Internal Revenue Service

Instructions for Form 2553
(Revised February 1986)
Election by a Small Business Corporation

(Section references are to the Internal Revenue Code, unless otherwise specified.)

Paperwork Reduction Act Notice.—We ask for this information to carry out the Internal Revenue laws of the United States. We need it to insure that you are complying with these laws and to allow us to figure and collect the right amount of tax. You are required to give us this information.

A. Purpose.—To elect to be treated as an "S Corporation," a corporation must file Form 2553. The election permits the income of the S corporation to be taxed to the shareholders of the corporation except as provided in Subchapter S and section 58(d). (See section 1363.)

B. Who May Elect.—Your corporation may make the election only if it meets the following tests:

1. It is a domestic corporation.

2. It has no more than 35 shareholders. A husband and wife (and their estates) are treated as one shareholder for this requirement. All other persons are treated as separate shareholders.

3. It has only individuals, estates, or certain trusts as shareholders.

4. It has no nonresident alien shareholders.

5. It has only one class of stock. See sections 1361(c)(4) and (5) for additional details.

6. It is not an ineligible corporation as defined in section 1361(b)(2). See section 6(c) of Public Law 97-354 for additional details.

7. It has a calendar tax year or other permitted tax year as explained in instruction G.

8. Each shareholder consents as explained in the instructions for Column D.

See sections 1361, 1362 and 1378 for additional information on the above tests.

C. Where to File.—File this election with the Internal Revenue Service Center where the corporation will file **Form 1120S**, U.S. Income Tax Return for an S Corporation. See the Instructions for Form 1120S for Service Center addresses.

You should keep a copy of Form 2553 for the corporation's files.

D. When to Make the Election.— Complete Form 2553 and file it either: (1) at any time during that portion of the first tax year the election is to take effect which occurs before the 16th day of the third month of that tax year (or at any time during that year, if that year does not extend beyond the period described above) or (2) in the tax year before the first tax year it is to take effect. An election made by a small business corporation after the 15th day of the third month but before the end of the tax year is treated as made for the next year. For example, if a calendar tax year corporation makes the election in April 1985, it is effective for the corporation's 1986 calendar tax year.

For purposes of this election, a newly formed corporation's tax year starts when it has shareholders, acquires assets, or begins doing business, whichever happens first.

E. Acceptance or Non-acceptance of Election.—IRS will notify you if your election is accepted and when it will take effect. You should generally receive determination on your election within 60 days after you have filed Form 2553. Do not file Form 1120S until you are notified that your election is accepted. If you are now required to file **Form 1120**, U.S. Corporation Income Tax Return, or any other applicable tax return, continue filing it until your election takes effect.

You will also be notified if your election is not accepted.

Care should be exercised to ensure the election is received by Internal Revenue Service. If you are not notified of acceptance or non-acceptance of your election within 3 months of date of filing (date mailed), you should take follow-up action by corresponding with the service center where the election was filed. If filing of Form 2553 is questioned, an acceptable proof of filing is: (1) Certified receipt (timely filed); (2) Form 2553 with accepted stamp; (3) Form 2553 with stamped IRS received date; or (4) IRS letter stating that Form 2553 had been accepted.

F. End of Election.—Once the election is made, it stays in effect for all years until it is terminated. During the 5 years after the election has been terminated, the corporation can make another election on Form 2553 only if the Commissioner consents. See section 1362(g). However, the 5-year waiting period does not apply to terminations made under Subchapter S rules in effect for tax years beginning before January 1, 1983. See sections 1362(d), (e), and (f) for rules regarding termination of election.

G. Permitted Tax Year.—Section 1378 provides that no corporation may make an election to be an S corporation for any tax year unless the tax year is a permitted tax year. A permitted tax year is a tax year ending December 31 or any other tax year for which the corporation establishes a business purpose to the satisfaction of IRS. See section 1378(c) if a 50 percent shift in ownership occurs in an existing S corporation after its election is made.

H. Investment Credit Property.— Although the corporation has elected to be an S corporation under section 1362, the tax imposed by section 47 in the case of early disposition of investment credit property will be imposed on the corporation for credits allowed for tax years for which the corporation was not an S corporation. The election will not be treated as a disposition of the property by the corporation. See section 1371(d).

Specific Instructions

Part I.—Part I must be completed by all corporations.

Name and Address of Corporation.—If the corporation's mailing address is the same as someone else's such as a shareholder's, please enter this person's name below the corporation's name.

Employer Identification Number.—If you have applied for an employer identification number (EIN) but have not received it, enter "applied for." If the corporation does not have an EIN, you should apply for one on **Form SS-4**, Application for Employer Identification Number, available from most IRS or Social Security Administration offices. Send Form SS-4 to the IRS Service Center where Form 1120S will be filed.

Principal Business Activity and Principal Product or Service.—Use the Codes for Principal Business Activity contained in the Instructions for Form 1120S. Your principal business activity is the one that accounts for the largest percentage of total receipts. Total receipts are gross receipts plus all other income.

Also state the principal product or service. For example, if the principal business activity is "grain mill products," the principal product or service may be "cereal preparation."

Number of Shares Issued and Outstanding.—Enter only one figure. This figure will be the number of shares of stock that have been issued to shareholders and have not been reacquired by the corporation. This is the number of shares all shareholders own, as reported in column E, Part I.

Item B.—The selected tax year must be a permitted tax year as defined in instruction G.

A newly formed corporation may automatically adopt a tax year ending December 31.

Generally, an existing corporation may automatically change to a tax year ending December 31, if all of its principal shareholders have tax years ending December 31, or if all of its principal shareholders are concurrently changing to such tax year. If a corporation is automatically changing to a tax year ending December 31, it is not necessary for the corporation to file **Form 1128**, Application for Change in Accounting Period. A shareholder may not change his or her tax year without securing prior approval from IRS. For purposes of the automatic change, a principal shareholder is a shareholder who owns 5% or more of the issued and outstanding stock of the corporation. See temporary regulations section 18.1378-1 for additional details.

If a corporation wants to change to a tax year ending December 31, but does not qualify for an automatic change as explained above, it may want to complete Part IV and indicate in an attached statement that it wants to change to a tax year ending December 31.

If a corporation selects a tax year ending other than December 31, it must complete Part II or IV in addition to Part I.

Column D.—Shareholders' Consent Statement.—Each person who is a shareholder at the time the election is made must consent to the election. If the election is made during the corporation's first tax year for which it is effective, any person who held stock at any time during that portion of that year which occurs before the time the election is made must consent to the election although the person may have sold or transferred his or her stock before the election is made. Each shareholder consents by signing in column D or signing a separate consent statement, described below.

The election by a small business corporation is considered made for the following tax year if one or more of the persons who held stock at any time during that portion of that year which occurs before the time the election is made did not consent to the election. See section 1362(b)(2).

If a husband and wife have a community interest in the stock or in the income from it, both must consent. Each tenant in common, joint tenant, and tenant by the entirety also must consent.

A minor's consent is made by the minor or the legal guardian. If no legal guardian has been appointed, the natural guardian makes the consent (even if a custodian holds the minor's stock under a law patterned after the Uniform Gifts to Minors Act).

Continuation Sheet or Separate Consent Statement.—If you need a continuation sheet or use a separate consent statement, attach it to Form 2553. The separate consent statement must contain the name, address, and employer identification number of the corporation and the shareholder information requested in columns C through G of Part I.

If you wish, you may combine all the shareholders' consents in one statement.

Column E.—Enter the number of shares of stock each shareholder owns and the dates the stock was acquired. If the election is made during the corporation's first tax year for which it is effective, do not list the shares of stock for those shareholders who sold or transferred all of their stock before the election was made but who still must consent to the election for it to be effective for the tax year.

Column G.—Enter the month and day that each shareholder's tax year ends. If a shareholder is changing his or her tax year, enter the tax year the shareholder is changing to. If the election is made during the corporation's first tax year for which it is effective, you do not have to enter the tax year of shareholders who sold or transferred all of their stock before the election was made but who still must consent to the election for it to be effective for the tax year.

Signature.—Form 2553 must be signed by the president, treasurer, assistant treasurer, chief accounting officer, or other corporate officer (such as tax officer) authorized to sign.

Part II.—Items H and I of Part II are to be completed by a corporation that selects a tax year ending other than December 31, and that qualifies under section 4.02, 4.03, or 4.04 of Revenue Procedure 83-25, 1983-1 C.B. 689. Items H and I are completed in place of the additional statement asked for in section 7.01 of the procedure. Sections 4.02, 4.03, and 4.04 provide for expeditious approval of certain corporations' requests to adopt, retain, or change to a tax year ending other than December 31. The representation statements in Part II of Form 2553 highlight the three types of requests provided for in the revenue procedure. A corporation adopting, retaining, or changing its accounting period under the procedure must comply with or satisfy all conditions of the procedure.

The revenue procedure applies only to the tax years of corporations which are electing S corporation status by filing Form 2553. A corporation is permitted to adopt, retain, or change its tax year only once under the procedure. It is not necessary for the corporation to file Form 1128 when adopting or changing its tax year under the procedure.

Items H and J of Part II are to be completed by a corporation that is making a request as specified in section 8 of the procedure. Section 8 provides that if a corporation wants to adopt, retain, or change to a tax year not specified under section 4.02, 4.03, or 4.04 of the procedure or certain paragraphs of temporary regulations section 18.1378-1, it should attach a statement to Form 2553 pursuant to the ruling request requirements of Revenue Procedure 85-1, 1985-1 C.B. 404. (Changes to this revenue procedure are usually incorporated annually into a new revenue procedure as the first revenue procedure of the year.) The statement must show the business purpose for the desired tax year.

Approval of tax year selections made under section 4.02, 4.03, or 4.04 of Revenue Procedure 83-25 are generally automatic; however, a request under section 8 is not automatic. If a request is made under section 8, the corporation may want to make the back-up request under Part III. See section 8 of the procedure for details.

Part III.—Check the box in Part III to make the back-up request provided by temporary regulations section 18.1378-1(b)(2)(ii)(A). This section provides that corporations requesting to retain (or adopt) a tax year ending other than December 31, may make a back-up request to adopt or change to a tax year ending December 31, in case the initial request for a fiscal year is denied. In order to make the back-up request, a corporation requesting to retain its tax year ending other than December 31, must qualify for an automatic change of its tax year under temporary regulations section 18.1378-1(b)(1).

Part IV.—Check the box in Part IV to request the IRS to determine your permitted tax year under the provisions of temporary regulations section 18.1378-1(d). If you check the box in Part IV, enter "See Part IV" in the space in item B, Part I, for month and year.

You may attach a schedule to Form 2553 showing any additional information you want the IRS to consider in making the determination. IRS will notify you of the permitted tax year determination. The tax year determination by IRS is final.

Form **2553**	**Election by a Small Business Corporation**	OMB No. 1545-0146
(Rev. February 1986) Department of the Treasury Internal Revenue Service	(Under section 1362 of the Internal Revenue Code) ► For Paperwork Reduction Act Notice, see page 1 of instructions. ► See separate instructions.	Expires 1-31-89

Note: *This election, to be treated as an "S corporation," can be approved only if all the tests in Instruction B are met.*

Part I   Election Information

Name of corporation (see instructions) ABC Corporation John Smith	Employer identification number (see instructions) 51-3657893	Principal business activity and principal product or service (see instructions) 7310- Advertising
Number and street 1 Main Street		Election is to be effective for tax year beginning (month, day, year) 1/1/89
City or town, state and ZIP code New York, NY 10003		Number of shares issued and outstanding (see instructions) 100

Is the corporation the outgrowth or continuation of any form of predecessor? . . . . ☐ Yes ☒ No

If "Yes," state name of predecessor, type of organization, and period of its existence ► ---------------------

Date and place of incorporation
6/1/88   DE

A If this election takes effect for the first tax year the corporation exists, enter the earliest of the following: (1) date the corporation first had shareholders, (2) date the corporation first had assets, or (3) date the corporation began doing business. ►   6/1/88

B Selected tax year: Annual return will be filed for tax year ending (month and day) ► December 31

See instructions before entering your tax year. If the tax year ends any date other than December 31, you must complete Part II or Part IV on back. You may want to complete Part III to make a back-up request.

C Name of each shareholder, person having a community property interest in the corporation's stock, and each tenant in common, joint tenant, and tenant by the entirety. (A husband and wife (and their estates) are counted as one shareholder in determining the number of shareholders without regard to the manner in which the stock is owned.)	D Shareholders' Consent Statement. We, the undersigned shareholders, consent to the corporation's election to be treated as an "S corporation" under section 1362(a). (Shareholders sign and date below.)*	E Stock owned		F Social security number (employer identification number for estates or trust)	G Tax year ends (month and day)
		Number of shares	Dates acquired		
John Smith	*John Smith*	20	6/1/88	222-88-5555	Dec. 31
Joan Jones	*Joan Jones*	20	6/1/88	222-99-6666	Dec. 31
Ken Brown	*Ken Brown*	20	6/1/88	222-66-4444	Dec. 31
Michael Green	*Michael Green*	20	6/1/88	222-33-1111	Dec. 31
Helen Williams	*Helen Williams*	20	6/1/88	222-55-7777	Dec. 31

*For this election to be valid, the consent of each shareholder, person having a community property interest in the corporation's stock, and each tenant in common, joint tenant, and tenant by the entirety must either appear above or be attached to this form. (See instructions for Column D, if continuation sheet or a separate consent statement is needed.)

Under penalties of perjury, I declare that I have examined this election, including accompanying schedules, and statements, and to the best of my knowledge and belief, it is true, correct, and complete.

Signature and Title of Officer ► *Ralph Johnson, President*	Date ► 7/1/88
See Parts II, III, and IV on back.	Form **2553** (Rev. 2-86)

Part II   Selection of Tax Year Under Revenue Procedure 83-25

H   Check the applicable box below to indicate whether the corporation is:

[X]   Adopting the tax year entered in item B, Part I.

[ ]   Retaining the tax year entered in item B, Part I.

[ ]   Changing to the tax year entered in item B, Part I.

I   Check the applicable box below to indicate the representation statement the corporation is making as required under section 7.01 (item 4) of Revenue Procedure 83-25, 1983-1 C.B. 689.

[X]   Under penalties of perjury, I represent that shareholders holding more than half of the shares of the stock (as of the first day of the tax year to which the request relates) of the corporation have the same tax year or are concurrently changing to the tax year that the corporation adopts, retains, or changes to per item B, Part I.

[ ]   Under penalties of perjury, I represent that shareholders holding more than half of the shares of the stock (as of the first day of the tax year to which the request relates) of the corporation have a tax year or are concurrently changing to a tax year that, although different from the tax year the corporation is adopting, retaining, or changing to per item B, Part I, results in a deferment of income to each of these shareholders of three months or less.

[ ]   Under penalties of perjury, I represent that the corporation is adopting, retaining, or changing to a tax year that coincides with its natural business year as verified by its satisfaction of the requirements of section 4.042(a), (b), (c), and (d) of Revenue Procedure 83-25.

J   Check here [ ] if the tax year entered in item B, Part I, is requested under the provisions of section 8 of Revenue Procedure 83-25. Attach to Form 2553 a statement and other necessary information pursuant to the ruling request requirements of Revenue Procedure 85-1. The statement must include the business purpose for the desired tax year. See instructions.

Part III   Back-Up Request by Certain Corporations Initially Selecting a Fiscal Year (See Instructions.)

Check here [ ] if the corporation agrees to adopt or to change to a tax year ending December 31 if necessary for IRS to accept this election for S corporation status (temporary regulations section 18.1378-1(b)(2)(ii)(A)). This back-up request does not apply if the fiscal tax year request is approved by IRS or if the election to be an S corporation is not accepted.

Part IV   Request by Corporation for Tax Year Determination by IRS (See Instructions.)

Check here [ ] if the corporation requests the IRS to determine the permitted tax year for the corporation based on information submitted in Part I (and attached schedules). This request is made under provisions of temporary regulations section 18.1378-1(d).

Form **2553**
(Rev. February 1986)

Department of the Treasury
Internal Revenue Service

Election by a Small Business Corporation

(Under section 1362 of the Internal Revenue Code)
▶ For Paperwork Reduction Act Notice, see page 1 of instructions.
▶ See separate instructions.

OMB No. 1545-0146

Expires 1-31-89

Note: *This election, to be treated as an "S corporation," can be approved only if all the tests in Instruction B are met.*

Part I Election Information

Name of corporation (see instructions)	Employer identification number (see instructions)	Principal business activity and principal product or service (see instructions)
Number and street		Election is to be effective for tax year beginning (month, day, year)
City or town, state and ZIP code		Number of shares issued and outstanding (see instructions)

Is the corporation the outgrowth or continuation of any form of predecessor? . . . . ☐ **Yes** ☐ **No**

If "Yes," state name of predecessor, type of organization, and period of its existence ▶ -----------------------

Date and place of incorporation

A If this election takes effect for the first tax year the corporation exists, enter the earliest of the following: (1) date the corporation first had shareholders, (2) date the corporation first had assets, or (3) date the corporation began doing business. ▶

B Selected tax year: Annual return will be filed for tax year ending (month and day) ▶ ---

See instructions before entering your tax year. If the tax year ends any date other than December 31, you must complete Part II or Part IV on back. You may want to complete Part III to make a back-up request.

C Name of each shareholder, person having a community property interest in the corporation's stock, and each tenant in common, joint tenant, and tenant by the entirety. (A husband and wife (and their estates) are counted as one shareholder in determining the number of shareholders without regard to the manner in which the stock is owned.)	D Shareholders' Consent Statement. We, the undersigned shareholders, consent to the corporation's election to be treated as an "S corporation" under section 1362(a). (Shareholders sign and date below.)*	E Stock owned		F Social security number (employer identification number for estates or trust)	G Tax year ends (month and day)
		Number of shares	Dates acquired		

*For this election to be valid, the consent of each shareholder, person having a community property interest in the corporation's stock, and each tenant in common, joint tenant, and tenant by the entirety must either appear above or be attached to this form. (See instructions for Column D, if continuation sheet or a separate consent statement is needed.)

Under penalties of perjury, I declare that I have examined this election, including accompanying schedules, and statements, and to the best of my knowledge and belief, it is true, correct, and complete.

Signature and Title of Officer ▶

Date ▶

See Parts II, III, and IV on back.

Form **2553** (Rev. 2-86)

Part II   Selection of Tax Year Under Revenue Procedure 83-25

H   Check the applicable box below to indicate whether the corporation is:

☐ Adopting the tax year entered in item B, Part I.

☐ Retaining the tax year entered in item B, Part I.

☐ Changing to the tax year entered in item B, Part I.

I   Check the applicable box below to indicate the representation statement the corporation is making as required under section 7.01 (item 4) of Revenue Procedure 83-25, 1983-1 C.B. 689.

☐ Under penalties of perjury, I represent that shareholders holding more than half of the shares of the stock (as of the first day of the tax year to which the request relates) of the corporation have the same tax year or are concurrently changing to the tax year that the corporation adopts, retains, or changes to per item B, Part I.

☐ Under penalties of perjury, I represent that shareholders holding more than half of the shares of the stock (as of the first day of the tax year to which the request relates) of the corporation have a tax year or are concurrently changing to a tax year that, although different from the tax year the corporation is adopting, retaining, or changing to per item B, Part I, results in a deferment of income to each of these shareholders of three months or less.

☐ Under penalties of perjury, I represent that the corporation is adopting, retaining, or changing to a tax year that coincides with its natural business year as verified by its satisfaction of the requirements of section 4.042(a), (b), (c), and (d) of Revenue Procedure 83-25.

J   Check here ☐ if the tax year entered in item B, Part I, is requested under the provisions of section 8 of Revenue Procedure 83-25. Attach to Form 2553 a statement and other necessary information pursuant to the ruling request requirements of Revenue Procedure 85-1. The statement must include the business purpose for the desired tax year. See instructions.

Part III   Back-Up Request by Certain Corporations Initially Selecting a Fiscal Year (See Instructions.)

Check here ☐ if the corporation agrees to adopt or to change to a tax year ending December 31 if necessary for IRS to accept this election for S corporation status (temporary regulations section 18.1378-1(b)(2)(ii)(A)). This back-up request does not apply if the fiscal tax year request is approved by IRS or if the election to be an S corporation is not accepted.

Part IV   Request by Corporation for Tax Year Determination by IRS (See Instructions.)

Check here ☐ if the corporation requests the IRS to determine the permitted tax year for the corporation based on information submitted in Part I (and attached schedules). This request is made under provisions of temporary regulations section 18.1378-1(d).

☆ U.S.G.P.O.: 1986–491–473/20122

NONPROFIT CORPORATIONS

SECTION XVII

A nonprofit corporation is special type of corporation formed for charitable and other purposes that are not profit seeking. It has many of the features of standard corporations with the major exception being its tax status.

The number of nonprofit corporations in the United States is remarkable, running into the hundreds of thousands. In some states like Ohio and New York, over one-third of all corporations chartered there are nonprofit. While there are critics of the growing phenomenon of the nonprofit corporation, in some towns and cities over 50% of the property is tax exempt. However, as long as the minimal requirements of IRS are met, it is legal under existing law and it is likely to keep expanding and growing.

Nonprofit corporations* do not issue stock. Instead membership certificates are often used. The form for a non stock, nonprofit corporation that is recommended for use is on the following page. It can be completed in the same way as the earlier certificates in this book and either mailed directly to the Secretary of State or through a registered agent.

Some individuals utilize nonprofit corporations as a tax shelter. Many corporate situations lend themselves to this tax exempt status. These endeavors can provide desirable tax advantages to the owner(s) of a corporation that may qualify for a government grant, to do research, educational experiments, etc.

A corporation can often qualify for tax exempt status and still pay its officers salaries and expenses. The salary and expenses may be questioned by the Internal Revenue Service on a tax audit if it is "excessive".

Other situations lending themselves to a nonprofit status are religious, fraternal and civic clubs. Also neighborhood associations often incorporate as a nonprofit corporation primarily to gain personal liability protection for its members.

Still another is when a person or group of persons create a nonprofit foundation for variants of charitable purposes such as for medical research.

Often a person's will can be worded so as to leave such assets as a list of stockholdings, or insurance proceeds (by insurance contract) to a nonprofit corporation that was organized by that person while still alive.

Since personal contributions to many nonprofit corporations are tax deductible, many tax exempt corporations utilize this incentive to obtain substantial funds often running into the millions of dollars for its operations. There are many fund raising firms that have organized to help nonprofit corporations with fund raising.

Owners of a nonprofit corporation should contact an Internal Revenue office and obtain forms to qualify for tax exempt status. See IRS booklet No. 557.

---

*More detailed information on this subject can be found in **Complete Non-Profit Corporation Handbook** , by Ted Nicholas $69.95, Enterprise Publishing, Inc., Dept. CB94J, 725 North Market Street, Wilmington, DE 19801. (This book also contains all necessary forms.)

Non-stock   Non-profit

CERTIFICATE OF INCORPORATION
of

Associated Charities, Inc.
_____

FIRST: The name of this corporation is_____ Associated Charities, Inc.
_____

SECOND: Its registered office in the State of Delaware is to be located at 725 North Market Street in the City of Wilmington, County of New Castle. The registered agent in charge thereof is The Company Corporation at the same address.

THIRD: The nature of the business and the objects and purposes proposed to be transacted, promoted and carried on, are to do any and all the things herein mentioned, as fully and to the same extent as natural persons might or could do, and in any part of the world, vis:

This is a non-stock, non-profit corporation. The purpose of the corporation is to engage in any lawful act or activity for which non-profit corporations may be organized under the General Corporation Law of Delaware.

Said corporation is organized exclusively for charitable, religious, education, and scientific purposes, including, for such purposes, the making of distributions to organizations that qualify as exempt organizations under Section 501(c)(3) of the Internal Revenue Code of 1954 (or the corresponding provision of any future United States Internal Revenue Law), to wit:

(In this space you may wish to include a statement describing the purpose and objectives of the corporation in more specific terms.)

FOURTH: The corporation shall not have any capital stock and the conditions of membership shall be stated in the Bylaws.

FIFTH: The name and mailing address of the incorporator is: _____
_____

(Leave blank if using The Company Corporation as your registered agent.)

SIXTH: The powers of the incorporator are to terminate upon filing of the Certificate of Incorporation, and the name(s) and mailing address(es) of the persons who are to serve as director(s) until their successors are elected are as follows:

Kathy Smith, 621 North Street, Anytown, Anystate 00000
_____

SEVENTH: The activities and affairs of the corporation shall be managed by a Board of Directors. The number of directors which shall constitute the whole Board shall be such as from time to time shall be fixed by, or in the manner provided in, the Bylaws, but in no case shall the number be less than one. The directors need not be members of the corporation unless so required by the Bylaws or by Statute. The Board of Directors shall be elected by the members at the annual meeting of the corporation to be held on such date as the Bylaws may provide, and shall hold office until their successors are respectively elected and qualified. The Bylaws shall specify the number of directors necessary to constitute a quorum. The Board of Directors may, by resolution or resolutions passed by a majority of the whole Board, designate one or more committees which, to the extent provided in said resolution or resolutions or in the Bylaws of the corporation, shall have and may exercise all the powers of the Board of Directors in the management of the activities and affairs of the corporation. They may further have power to authorize the seal of the corporation to be affixed to all papers which may require it; and such committee or committees shall have such name or names as may be stated in the Bylaws of the corporation or as may be determined from time to time

by resolution adopted by the Board of Directors. The directors of the corporation may, if the Bylaws so provide, be classified as to term of office. The corporation may elect such officers as the Bylaws may specify, subject to the provisions of the Statute, who shall have titles and exercise such duties as the Bylaws may provide. The Board of Directors is expressly authorized to make, alter, or repeal the Bylaws of this corporation. This corporation may in its Bylaws confer powers upon its Board of Directors in addition to the foregoing, and in addition to the powers and authorities expressly conferred upon them by the Statute. This is true, provided that the Board of Directors shall not exercise any power of authority conferred herein or by Statute upon the members.

EIGHTH: Meetings of members may be held without the State of Delaware, if the Bylaws so provide. The books of the corporation may be kept (subject to any provisions contained in the Statutes) outside the State of Delaware at such place or places as may be from time to time designated by the Board of Directors.

NINTH: No part of the net earnings of the corporation shall inure to the benefit of, or be distributable to, its members, directors, officers or other private persons, except that the corporation shall be authorized and empowered to pay reasonable compensation for services rendered and to make payments and distributions in furtherance of the purposes set forth in Article Three hereof. No part of the activities of the corporation shall consist of the carrying on of propaganda, or otherwise attempting to intervene in (including the publishing or distribution of statements) any of these articles, the corporation shall not carry on any other activities not permitted to be carried on (a) by a corporation exempt from Federal Income Tax under Section 501(c)(3) of the Internal Revenue Code of 1954 (or the corresponding provision of any future United States Internal Revenue Law) or (b) by a corporation, contributions to which are deductible under Section 170(c)(2) of the Internal Revenue Code of 1954 (or the corresponding provision of any future United States Internal Revenue Law).

TENTH: Upon the dissolution of the corporation, the Board of Directors shall, after paying or making provisions for the payment of all of the liabilities of the corporation, dispose of all of the assets of the corporation exclusively for the purpose of the corporation in such manner, or to such organization or organizations and operated exclusively for charitable, educational, religious, or scientific purposes as shall at the time qualify as an exempt organization under Section 501(c)(3) of the Internal Revenue Code of 1954 (or the corresponding provision of any future United States Law) as the Board of Directors shall determine. Any such assets not so disposed of shall be disposed of by the Court of Common Pleas of the county in which the principal office of the corporation is then located, exclusively for such purposes or to such organization or organizations, as said Court shall determine, which are organized and operated exclusively for such designated purposes.

ELEVENTH: The corporation reserves the right to amend, alter, change or repeal any provision contained in this Certificate of Incorporation, in the manner now or hereafter prescribed by the Statute, and all rights conferred upon members herein are granted subject to their reservation.

TWELFTH: Directors of the corporation shall not be liable to either the corporation or its members for monetary damages for a breach of fiduciary duties unless the breach involves: (1) a director's duty of loyalty to the corporation or its members; (2) acts or omissions not in good faith or which involve intentional misconduct or a knowing violation of law; (3) a transaction from which the director derived an improper personal benefit.

I. THE UNDERSIGNED, being each of the incorporators hereinbefore named, for the purpose of forming a non-profit corporation pursuant to Chapter 1 of Title 8 of the Delaware Code, do make this certificate, hereby declaring and certifying that the facts herein stated are true, and accordingly have hereunto set my hand this

_____14th_____ day of _____June_____ A.D. 19 _xx_ .

_____John Doe_____
(Signature of Incorporator. Leave blank if TCC is your registered agent.)

Non-stock

Non-profit

CERTIFICATE OF INCORPORATION
of

_____

FIRST: The name of this corporation is _____

_____

SECOND: Its registered office in the State of Delaware is to be located at 725 North Market Street in the City of Wilmington, County of New Castle. The registered agent in charge thereof is The Company Corporation at the same address.

THIRD: The nature of the business and the objects and purposes proposed to be transacted, promoted and carried on, are to do any and all the things herein mentioned, as fully and to the same extent as natural persons might or could do, and in any part of the world, vis:

This is a non-stock, non-profit corporation. The purpose of the corporation is to engage in any lawful act or activity for which non-profit corporations may be organized under the General Corporation Law of Delaware.

Said corporation is organized exclusively for charitable, religious, education, and scientific purposes, including, for such purposes, the making of distributions to organizations that qualify as exempt organizations under Section 501(c)(3) of the Internal Revenue Code of 1954 (or the corresponding provision of any future United States Internal Revenue Law), to wit:

FOURTH: The corporation shall not have any capital stock and the conditions of membership shall be stated in the Bylaws.

FIFTH: The name and mailing address of the incorporator is: _____

_____

SIXTH: The powers of the incorporator are to terminate upon filing of the Certificate of Incorporation, and the name(s) and mailing address(es) of the persons who are to serve as director(s) until their successors are elected are as follows:

_____

_____

SEVENTH: The activities and affairs of the corporation shall be managed by a Board of Directors. The number of directors which shall constitute the whole Board shall be such as from time to time shall be fixed by, or in the manner provided in, the Bylaws, but in no case shall the number be less than one. The directors need not be members of the corporation unless so required by the Bylaws or by Statute. The Board of Directors shall be elected by the members at the annual meeting of the corporation to be held on such date as the Bylaws may provide, and shall hold office until their successors are respectively elected and qualified. The Bylaws shall specify the number of directors necessary to constitute a quorum. The Board of Directors may, by resolution or resolutions passed by a majority of the whole Board, designate one or more committees which, to the extent provided in said resolution or resolutions or in the Bylaws of the corporation, shall have and may exercise all the powers of the Board of Directors in the management of the activities and affairs of the corporation. They may further have power to authorize the seal of the corporation to be affixed to all papers which may require it; and such committee or committees shall have such name or names as may be stated in the Bylaws of the corporation or as may be determined from time to time

by resolution adopted by the Board of Directors. The directors of the corporation may, if the Bylaws so provide, be classified as to term of office. The corporation may elect such officers as the Bylaws may specify, subject to the provisions of the Statute, who shall have titles and exercise such duties as the Bylaws may provide. The Board of Directors is expressly authorized to make, alter, or repeal the Bylaws of this corporation. This corporation may in its Bylaws confer powers upon its Board of Directors in addition to the foregoing, and in addition to the powers and authorities expressly conferred upon them by the Statute. This is true, provided that the Board of Directors shall not exercise any power of authority conferred herein or by Statute upon the members.

EIGHTH: Meetings of members may be held without the State of Delaware, if the Bylaws so provide. The books of the corporation may be kept (subject to any provisions contained in the Statutes) outside the State of Delaware at such place or places as may be from time to time designated by the Board of Directors.

NINTH: No part of the net earnings of the corporation shall inure to the benefit of, or be distributable to, its members, directors, officers or other private persons, except that the corporation shall be authorized and empowered to pay reasonable compensation for services rendered and to make payments and distributions in furtherance of the purposes set forth in Article Three hereof. No part of the activities of the corporation shall consist of the carrying on of propaganda, or otherwise attempting to intervene in (including the publishing or distribution of statements) any of these articles, the corporation shall not carry on any other activities not permitted to be carried on (a) by a corporation exempt from Federal Income Tax under Section 501(c)(3) of the Internal Revenue Code of 1954 (or the corresponding provision of any future United States Internal Revenue Law) or (b) by a corporation, contributions to which are deductible under Section 170(c)(2) of the Internal Revenue Code of 1954 (or the corresponding provision of any future United States Internal Revenue Law).

TENTH: Upon the dissolution of the corporation, the Board of Directors shall, after paying or making provisions for the payment of all of the liabilities of the corporation, dispose of all of the assets of the corporation exclusively for the purpose of the corporation in such manner, or to such organization or organizations and operated exclusively for charitable, educational, religious, or scientific purposes as shall at the time qualify as an exempt organization under Section 501(c)(3) of the Internal Revenue Code of 1954 (or the corresponding provision of any future United States Law) as the Board of Directors shall determine. Any such assets not so disposed of shall be disposed of by the Court of Common Pleas of the county in which the principal office of the corporation is then located, exclusively for such purposes or to such organization or organizations, as said Court shall determine, which are organized and operated exclusively for such designated purposes.

ELEVENTH: The corporation reserves the right to amend, alter, change or repeal any provision contained in this Certificate of Incorporation, in the manner now or hereafter prescribed by the Statute, and all rights conferred upon members herein are granted subject to their reservation.

TWELFTH: Directors of the corporation shall not be liable to either the corporation or its members for monetary damages for a breach of fiduciary duties unless the breach involves: (1) a director's duty of loyalty to the corporation or its members; (2) acts or omissions not in good faith or which involve intentional misconduct or a knowing violation of law; (3) a transaction from which the director derived an improper personal benefit.

I. THE UNDERSIGNED, being each of the incorporators hereinbefore named, for the purpose of forming a non-profit corporation pursuant to Chapter 1 of Title 8 of the Delaware Code, do make this certificate, hereby declaring and certifying that the facts herein stated are true, and accordingly have hereunto set my hand this

_____ day of _____ A.D. 19_____ .

_____

Non-stock   Non-profit

CERTIFICATE OF INCORPORATION
of

_____

FIRST: The name of this corporation is _____

_____

SECOND: Its registered office in the State of Delaware is to be located at 725 North Market Street in the City of Wilmington, County of New Castle. The registered agent in charge thereof is The Company Corporation at the same address.

THIRD: The nature of the business and the objects and purposes proposed to be transacted, promoted and carried on, are to do any and all the things herein mentioned, as fully and to the same extent as natural persons might or could do, and in any part of the world, vis:

This is a non-stock, non-profit corporation. The purpose of the corporation is to engage in any lawful act or activity for which non-profit corporations may be organized under the General Corporation Law of Delaware.

Said corporation is organized exclusively for charitable, religious, education, and scientific purposes, including, for such purposes, the making of distributions to organizations that qualify as exempt organizations under Section 501(c)(3) of the Internal Revenue Code of 1954 (or the corresponding provision of any future United States Internal Revenue Law), to wit:

FOURTH: The corporation shall not have any capital stock and the conditions of membership shall be stated in the Bylaws.

FIFTH: The name and mailing address of the incorporator is: _____

_____

SIXTH: The powers of the incorporator are to terminate upon filing of the Certificate of Incorporation, and the name(s) and mailing address(es) of the persons who are to serve as director(s) until their successors are elected are as follows:

_____

_____

SEVENTH: The activities and affairs of the corporation shall be managed by a Board of Directors. The number of directors which shall constitute the whole Board shall be such as from time to time shall be fixed by, or in the manner provided in, the Bylaws, but in no case shall the number be less than one. The directors need not be members of the corporation unless so required by the Bylaws or by Statute. The Board of Directors shall be elected by the members at the annual meeting of the corporation to be held on such date as the Bylaws may provide, and shall hold office until their successors are respectively elected and qualified. The Bylaws shall specify the number of directors necessary to constitute a quorum. The Board of Directors may, by resolution or resolutions passed by a majority of the whole Board, designate one or more committees which, to the extent provided in said resolution or resolutions or in the Bylaws of the corporation, shall have and may exercise all the powers of the Board of Directors in the management of the activities and affairs of the corporation. They may further have power to authorize the seal of the corporation to be affixed to all papers which may require it; and such committee or committees shall have such name or names as may be stated in the Bylaws of the corporation or as may be determined from time to time

by resolution adopted by the Board of Directors. The directors of the corporation may, if the Bylaws so provide, be classified as to term of office. The corporation may elect such officers as the Bylaws may specify, subject to the provisions of the Statute, who shall have titles and exercise such duties as the Bylaws may provide. The Board of Directors is expressly authorized to make, alter, or repeal the Bylaws of this corporation. This corporation may in its Bylaws confer powers upon its Board of Directors in addition to the foregoing, and in addition to the powers and authorities expressly conferred upon them by the Statute. This is true, provided that the Board of Directors shall not exercise any power of authority conferred herein or by Statute upon the members.

EIGHTH: Meetings of members may be held without the State of Delaware, if the Bylaws so provide. The books of the corporation may be kept (subject to any provisions contained in the Statutes) outside the State of Delaware at such place or places as may be from time to time designated by the Board of Directors.

NINTH: No part of the net earnings of the corporation shall inure to the benefit of, or be distributable to, its members, directors, officers or other private persons, except that the corporation shall be authorized and empowered to pay reasonable compensation for services rendered and to make payments and distributions in furtherance of the purposes set forth in Article Three hereof. No part of the activities of the corporation shall consist of the carrying on of propaganda, or otherwise attempting to intervene in (including the publishing or distribution of statements) any of these articles, the corporation shall not carry on any other activities not permitted to be carried on (a) by a corporation exempt from Federal Income Tax under Section 501(c)(3) of the Internal Revenue Code of 1954 (or the corresponding provision of any future United States Internal Revenue Law) or (b) by a corporation, contributions to which are deductible under Section 170(c)(2) of the Internal Revenue Code of 1954 (or the corresponding provision of any future United States Internal Revenue Law).

TENTH: Upon the dissolution of the corporation, the Board of Directors shall, after paying or making provisions for the payment of all of the liabilities of the corporation, dispose of all of the assets of the corporation exclusively for the purpose of the corporation in such manner, or to such organization or organizations and operated exclusively for charitable, educational, religious, or scientific purposes as shall at the time qualify as an exempt organization under Section 501(c)(3) of the Internal Revenue Code of 1954 (or the corresponding provision of any future United States Law) as the Board of Directors shall determine. Any such assets not so disposed of shall be disposed of by the Court of Common Pleas of the county in which the principal office of the corporation is then located, exclusively for such purposes or to such organization or organizations, as said Court shall determine, which are organized and operated exclusively for such designated purposes.

ELEVENTH: The corporation reserves the right to amend, alter, change or repeal any provision contained in this Certificate of Incorporation, in the manner now or hereafter prescribed by the Statute, and all rights conferred upon members herein are granted subject to their reservation.

TWELFTH: Directors of the corporation shall not be liable to either the corporation or its members for monetary damages for a breach of fiduciary duties unless the breach involves: (1) a director's duty of loyalty to the corporation or its members; (2) acts or omissions not in good faith or which involve intentional misconduct or a knowing violation of law; (3) a transaction from which the director derived an improper personal benefit.

I. THE UNDERSIGNED, being each of the incorporators hereinbefore named, for the purpose of forming a non-profit corporation pursuant to Chapter 1 of Title 8 of the Delaware Code, do make this certificate, hereby declaring and certifying that the facts herein stated are true, and accordingly have hereunto set my hand this

_____ day of _____ A.D. 19_____

_____

PROFESSIONAL CORPORATIONS

SECTION XVIII

Professionals in some of the United States may be able to take advantage of the benefits of Delaware Corporate Laws.

The same form as for a business corporation is usable by a professional. Professionals should add the initials "P.A." (Professional Association) or "P.C." (Professional Corporation) to the corporate title on the certificate of incorporation, i.e., Jones & Smith, (P.A.). The words Inc., etc., do not appear.

However, professionals such as doctors, dentists, architects, lawyers, etc. are treated differently under the law than are business corporations due to the nature of the professional's activities (the term "professional" here relates to a person providing a service for which a license is required).

In order to assure that the corporation status for the professional is not disallowed for tax purposes, the corporation that is engaged in the business of providing professional service must—

A.   Be owned by professionals of the same field and within the same professional practice (within the same office).

B.   Make provisions by agreement to leave stock to other professionals in the same profession and within the same practice and have a purchase agreement in the event of death with the same provisions.

C.   Not engage in any other business or activity with a professional in the same practice or investment of any kind other than that of providing the primary professional service such as dentistry, etc.

D.   Make certain that the professional relationship between the person furnishing the professional service and the person receiving it does not eliminate the personal liability of the professional for misconduct or negligence.

NOTE: Since the corporate laws from state to state vary greatly with regard to professionals, it is advisable to write the Secretary of State in the state where the professional practices to obtain any other provisions that should be included in the records of this type of Delaware corporation.

Some states have licensing requirements *that do not permit* (particularly physicians) a professional corporation to be formed *out of state*; so that a Delaware professional corporation is only possible for professionals licensed in Delaware. In order to be completely safe, a professional should request an opinion in writing of the *licensing* department of that state *before* proceeding with the formation of a Delaware Corporation.

FOR ADDITIONAL INFORMATION

SECTION XIX

To obtain a complete copy of the Delaware Corporation Law, write to The Company Corporation, Corporation Center, 725 North Market Street, Wilmington, Delaware 19801, and send $19.95, includes postage and handling. This publication completely outlines the entire corporation law. The writing is cumbersome. Nevertheless, it is well indexed and gives various kinds of helpful information.

If a reader wishes to make an interesting comparison between the advantages of Delaware Corporation Laws versus those of any other state, he may write the Secretary of State, c/o Corporation Department of any state and request information on obtaining a copy of the corporation laws.

CORPORATIONS FORMED IN STATES OTHER THAN DELAWARE

SECTION XX

A corporation in existence and formed in any state other than Delaware may wish to register to do business in Delaware.

On the next page is a specimen Foreign Corporation Certificate. An official of the "foreign" corporation (foreign to Delaware) may complete the form. A Registered Agent in Delaware must be appointed. (The Company Corporation will forward the form to the Secretary of State and act as Registered Agent for an initial annual fee of $35.) The Registered Agent then files the form with the Secretary of State, Dover, Delaware. The State Tax and fees covering the registration of a "foreign" corporation are $85.00. This approach applies best when a non-Delaware corporation wants to register to do business in Delaware. However, there is an approach to obtaining all the benefits of Delaware Corporate Law which the above does not accomplish. This method is favored by more and more corporations. This includes large corporations as well as one-man or family corporations. The objective to the following approach here is to arrange for an existing corporation to obtain the advantages of Delaware Corporate Laws.

A new Delaware corporation is formed and the non-Delaware corporation (i.e., a New York corporation) is merged into the new Delaware corporation. The Delaware fee for a merger is approximately $55.00, if both corporations have simple formats and no more stock is issued by the surviving Delaware corporation.

An agreement is made between the corporations that outlines the terms of the merger between the corporations which includes how many shares of the old corporation for how many shares of the new corporation is helpful. This agreement becomes part of the new corporation's records. After the agreement is completed, a Registered Agent can assist in filing the forms with the state.

To take advantage of Delaware Law, in almost all cases it pays to form a new Delaware corporation and merge the old one into the new one.

FOREIGN CORPORATION CERTIFICATE

THE UNDERSIGNED, a corporation duly organized and existing under the laws of the State of
, in accordance with the provisions of
Section 371 of Title 8 of the Delaware Code, does hereby certify:

FIRST: That
is a corporation duly organized and existing under the laws of the State of
and is filing herewith a certificate evidencing its corporate existence.

SECOND: That the name and address of its registered agent in said State of Delaware upon whom
service of process may be had is

THIRD: That the assets of said corporation are $ and that the liabilities thereof
are $. That the assets and liabilities indicated are as of a date within six months prior
to the filing date of this certificate.

FOURTH: That the business which it proposes to do in the State of Delaware is as follows:

FIFTH: That the business which it proposes to do in the State of Delaware is a business it is authorized
to do in the Jurisdiction of its Incorporation.

IN WITNESS WHEREOF, said Corporation has caused this Certificate to be signed on its behalf and
its corporate seal affixed this day of   , 19

(CORPORATE SEAL)

_____

_____
                              President

FOREIGN CORPORATION CERTIFICATE

THE UNDERSIGNED, a corporation duly organized and existing under the laws of the State of
, in accordance with the provisions of
Section 371 of Title 8 of the Delaware Code, does hereby certify:

FIRST: That
is a corporation duly organized and existing under the laws of the State of
and is filing herewith a certificate evidencing its corporate existence.

SECOND: That the name and address of its registered agent in said State of Delaware upon whom service of process may be had is

THIRD: That the assets of said corporation are $ and that the liabilities thereof are $. That the assets and liabilities indicated are as of a date within six months prior to the filing date of this certificate.

FOURTH: That the business which it proposes to do in the State of Delaware is as follows:

FIFTH: That the business which it proposes to do in the State of Delaware is a business it is authorized to do in the Jurisdiction of its Incorporation.

IN WITNESS WHEREOF, said Corporation has caused this Certificate to be signed on its behalf and its corporate seal affixed this day of   , 19

(CORPORATE SEAL)

_____

_____
President

MINUTES, BY-LAWS, ARTICLES OF INCORPORATION
STANDARD FORMS, REVIEW

SECTION XXI

On the following pages are all the forms necessary for a new corporation to have. For those incorporating who are not utilizing the services of a registered agent, this book contains necessary forms in blank that may be removed and used. All that is needed is for these forms to be completed by filling in the blanks (the only items that are desirable for a corporation to have that are not included in this book are the corporate seal and stock certificates. These can be purchased through a stationery store or through The Company Corporation as a complete bound set of the corporate forms).

A review of the procedure in forming a Delaware corporation without the services of a registered agent is:

1. Arrange to obtain Delaware street mailing address, if practical.

2. File Certificate of Incorporation with the Secretary of State in Dover, Delaware.

3. When the Certificate is returned from the Secretary of State, file a copy with the Recorder of Deeds office using the Delaware mailing address.

4. Instead of using the forms which can be supplied in a "kit" by a registered agent, tear out forms on following pages.

5. Fill in the blanks on those forms with appropriate information. Keep these forms with the corporate records. From time to time, keep a record of any meeting the Director(s) has by using these forms and filling in the blanks.

6. If desirable, buy stock certificates (either printed or unprinted) from a stationery store.

7. Purchase a corporate seal. This can also be purchased at a stationery store.

A list of forms* included follows:

A. Statement of Incorporator in lieu of Organization Meeting. This form may be used in all cases and all types of Corporations. Signature(s) same as appear on Certificate of Incorporation.

B. First Meeting of Directors. Complete and use only if there is more than one director. This form does not need to be used if the corporation is a close corporation.

C. Waiver of Notice. Complete and use only if there is more than one director.

D. Organization Meeting Form. Complete and use only if there is no more than one director. One person holds all offices. This form does not need to be used if the corporation is a close corporation.

E. By-Laws and Articles of Incorporation. Complete and use in all cases and keep with the corporate records.

NOTE: *Do not send any of the following forms to your registered agent. They are to be kept with your corporate records.*

---

* *Forms reprinted with permission of Excelsior-Legal Stationery Co., Inc.*

STATEMENT BY INCORPORATOR(S) OF ACTION TAKEN
IN LIEU OF ORGANIZATION MEETING OF

_____

The undersigned being the incorporator(s) of the corporation make the following statement of action taken to organize the corporation in lieu of an organization meeting.

By-laws regulating the conduct of the business and affairs of the corporation were adopted and appended to this statement.

The following person(s) were appointed director(s) of the corporation until the first annual meeting of the stockholders or until their successors shall be elected or appointed and shall qualify:

The director(s) were authorized and directed to issue from time to time the shares of capital stock of the corporation, now or hereafter authorized, wholly or partly for cash, or labor done, or services performed, or for personal property, or real property or leases thereof, received for the use and lawful purposes of the corporation, or for any consideration permitted by law, as in the discretion of the director(s) may seem for the best interests of the corporation.

_____

_____

_____

The following are to be appended to this statement:
Copy of the Certificate of Incorporation
By-Laws

The STATEMENT BY INCORPORATOR(S) OF ACTION TAKEN IN LIEU OF ORGANIZATION MEETING, together with a copy of the By-laws which were adopted in said statement, was then presented to the meeting by the secretary.

Thereupon, on motion duly made, seconded and unanimously carried, it was

RESOLVED, that the STATEMENT BY INCORPORATOR(S) OF ACTION TAKEN IN LIEU OF ORGANIZATION MEETING, dated   19   which has been presented to this meeting, be and hereby is in all respects approved, ratified and confirmed and further

RESOLVED, that the By-laws in the form adopted by the incorporator(s) in the aforementioned statement be and hereby are adopted as and for the By-laws of this corporation.

The secretary then presented and read to the meeting a copy of the certificate of incorporation of the corporation reported that on the day of   19   the original thereof was duly filed in the office of the Secretary of State and that a certified copy thereof was recorded on

19   in the office of the Recorder of the County of

Upon motion duly made, seconded and carried said report was adopted and the secretary was directed to append to these minutes a certified copy of the certificate of incorporation.

The chairman presented and read, article by article, the proposed by-laws for the conduct and regulation of the business and affairs of the corporation.

Upon motion duly made, seconded and carried, they were adopted and in all respects, ratified, confirmed and approved, as and for the By-laws of the corporation. The secretary was directed to cause them to be inserted in the minute book.

The secretary submitted to the meeting a seal proposed for use as the corporate seal of the corporation. Upon motion duly made, seconded and carried; it was

RESOLVED, that the seal now presented at this meeting, an impression of which is directed to be made in the margin of the minute book, be and the same hereby is adopted as the seal of the corporation.

The chairman then suggested that the secretary of the corporation be authorized to procure the necessary books and that the treasurer of the corporation be authorized to pay all expenses and to reimburse all persons for expenses made in connection with the organization of this corporation. After discussion, on motion duly made, seconded and unanimously carried, it was

RESOLVED, that the secretary of this corporation be and he hereby is authorized and directed to procure all corporate books, books of account and share certificate books required by the statutes of the State of Delaware or necessary or appropriate in connection with the business of this corporation; and it was further

RESOLVED, that the treasurer of this corporation be and he hereby is authorized to pay all charges and expenses incident to or arising out of the organization of this corporation and to reimburse any person who has made any disbursements therefor.

The secretary then presented to the meeting a proposed form of certificates for fully paid and non-assessable shares of stock of this corporation. The chairman directed that the specimen copy of such form of certificate be annexed to the minutes of the meeting. Upon motion duly made, seconded and unanimously carried it was

RESOLVED, that the form of certificate for fully paid and non-assessable shares of stock of this corporation submitted to this meeting, be and it hereby is adopted as the certificate to represent fully paid and non-assessable shares of stock and that a specimen of such certificate be annexed to the minutes of the meeting.

MINUTES OF THE FIRST MEETING OF
THE BOARD OF DIRECTORS OF

_____

    The first meeting of directors was held at

on the   day of   19   at   o'clock   M.

    The following were present:

being a quorum and all the directors of the corporation.

    One of the directors called the meeting to order. Upon motion duly made, seconded and carried,
was duly elected chairman of the meeting and
was duly elected secretary thereof. They
accepted their respective offices and proceeded with the discharge of their duties.

    A written waiver of notice of this meeting signed by the directors was submitted, read by the secretary and ordered appended to these minutes.

    The chairman stated that the election of officers was then in order.

    The following were duly nominated and, note having been taken, were unanimously elected officers of the corporation to serve for one year and until their successors are elected and qualified:

        President:

        Vice-President:

        Secretary:

        Treasurer:

    The president and secretary thereupon assumed their respective offices in place and stead of the temporary chairman and the temporary secretary.

WAIVER OF NOTICE OF THE FIRST MEETING OF
THE BOARD OF DIRECTORS OF

_____

We, the undersigned, being all the directors of the above corporation hereby agree and consent that the first meeting of the board be held on the date and at the time and place stated below for the purpose of electing officers and the transaction thereat of all such other business as may lawfully come before said meeting and hereby waive all notice of the meeting and of any adjournment thereof.

Place of meeting

Date of meeting

Time of meeting

_____
Director

_____
Director

_____
Director

Dated:

ORGANIZATION MINUTES OF THE SOLE DIRECTOR OF

_____

The undersigned, being the sole director of the corporation, organized under the General Corporation Law of Delaware, took the following action to organize the corporation and in furtherance of its business objectives on the date and at the place set forth below:

A certified copy of the Certificate of Incorporation filed in the office of the Secretary of State on
19   and recorded in the office of the Recorder of
the County of   19   was appended to these minutes.

The office of the corporation was fixed at
in the City of   State of

By-Laws regulating the conduct of the business and affairs of the corporation were adopted and appended to these minutes.

It was decided to issue from time to time all of the authorized shares of the capital stock of the corporation, now or hereafter authorized, wholly or partly for cash, for labor done, or services performed, or for personal property, or real property or leases thereof, received for the use and lawful purposes of the corporation, or for any consideration, permitted by law, as in the discretion of the director may seem for the best interest of the corporation.

The following were appointed officers of the corporation to serve for one year and until their successors were appointed or elected and qualified:

President: Secretary:

Vice-President: Treasurer:

Each officer thereupon assumed the duties of his office.

A written proposal from
addressed to the corporation and dated
pertaining to the issuance of the shares of the corporation was appended to minutes.

The following action was taken upon said proposal:

RESOLVED, that said proposal or offer be and the same hereby is approved and accepted and that in accordance with the terms thereof, the corporation issue to the offeror(s) or nominee(s)
fully paid and non-assessable shares of this corporation, and it is

RESOLVED, that upon the delivery to the corporation of said assets and the execution and delivery of such proper instruments as may be necessary to transfer and convey the same to the corporation, the officers of this corporation are authorized and directed to execute and deliver the certificates for such shares as are required to be issued and delivered on acceptance of said proposal in accordance with foregoing.

BY-LAWS
OF

_____

ARTICLE I — OFFICES

SECTION 1. REGISTERED OFFICE. — The registered office shall be established and maintained at

in the County of   in the State of Delaware.

SECTION 2. OTHER OFFICES. — The corporation may have other offices, either within or without the State of Delaware, at such place or places as the Board of Directors may from time to time appoint or the business of the corporation may require.

ARTICLE II — MEETING OF STOCKHOLDERS

SECTION 1. ANNUAL MEETINGS. — Annual meetings of stockholders for the election of directors and for such other business as may be stated in the notice of the meeting, shall be held at such place, either within or without the State of Delaware, and at such time and date as the Board of Directors, by resolution, shall determine and as set forth in the notice of the meeting. In the event the Board of Directors fails to so determine the time, date and place of the meeting, the annual meeting of stockholders shall be held at the registered office of the corporation in Delaware on

If the date of the annual meeting shall fall upon a legal holiday, the meeting shall be held on the next succeeding business day. At each annual meeting, the stockholders entitled to vote shall elect a Board of Directors and may transact such other corporate business as shall be stated in the notice of the meeting.

SECTION 2. OTHER MEETINGS. — Meetings of stockholders for any purpose other than the election of directors may be held at such time and place, within or without the State of Delaware, as shall be stated in the notice of the meeting.

SECTION 3. VOTING. — Each stockholder entitled to vote in accordance with the terms and provisions of the Certificate of Incorporation and these By-Laws shall be entitled to one vote, in person or by proxy, for each share of stock entitled to vote held by such stockholder, but no proxy shall be voted after three years from its date unless such proxy provides for a longer period. Upon the demand of any stockholder, the vote for directors and upon any question before the meeting shall be by ballot. All elections for directors shall be decided by plurality vote; all other questions shall be decided by majority vote except as otherwise provided by the Certificate of Incorporation or and laws of the State of Delaware.

SECTION 4. STOCKHOLDER LIST. — The officer who has charge of the stock ledger of the corporation shall at least 10 days before each meeting of stockholders prepare a complete alphabetically addressed list of the stockholders entitled to vote at the ensuing election, with the number of shares held by each. Said list shall be open to the examination of any stockholder, for any purpose germane to the meeting, during ordinary business hours, for a period of at least ten days prior to the meeting, either at a place within the city where the meeting is to be held, which place shall be specified in the notice of the meeting, or, if not specified, at the place where the meeting is to be held. The list shall be available for inspection at the meeting.

SECTION 5. QUORUM. — Except as otherwise required by law, by the Certificate of Incorporation or by these By-Laws, the presence, in person or by proxy, of stockholders holding a majority of the stock of the corporation entitled to vote shall constitute a meeting, a majority in interest of the stockholders entitled to vote thereat, present in person or by proxy, shall have power to adjourn the meeting from time to time, without notice other than announcement at the meeting, until the requisite amount of stock entitled to vote shall be present. At any such adjourned meeting at which the requisite amount of stock entitled to vote shall be represented, any business may be transacted which might have been transacted at the meeting as originally noticed; but only those stockholders entitled to vote at the meeting as originally noticed shall be entitled to vote at any adjournment or adjournments thereof.

SECTION 6. SPECIAL MEETING. — Special meeting of the stockholders, for any purpose, unless otherwise prescribed by statute or by the Certificate of Incorporation, may be called by the president and shall be called by the president or secretary at the request in writing of a majority of the directors or stockholders entitled to vote. Such request shall state the purpose of the proposed meeting.

SECTION 7. NOTICE OF MEETINGS. — Written notice, stating the place, date and time of the meeting, and the general nature of the business to be considered, shall be given to each stockholder entitled to vote thereat at his address as it appears on the records of the corporation, not less than ten nor more than fifty days before the date of the meeting.

SECTION 8. BUSINESS TRANSACTED. — No business other than that stated in the notice shall be transacted at any meeting without the unanimous consent of all the stockholders entitled to vote thereat.

SECTION 9. ACTION WITHOUT MEETING. — Except as otherwise provided by the Certificate of Incorporation, whenever the vote of stockholders at a meeting thereof is required or permitted to be taken in connection with any corporate action by any provisions of the statutes or the Certificate of Incorporation or of these By-Laws, the meeting and vote of stockholders may be dispensed with, if all the stockholders who would have been entitled to vote upon the action if such meeting were held shall consent in writing to such corporate action being taken.

ARTICLE III — DIRECTORS

SECTION 1. NUMBER AND TERM. — The number of directors shall be   . The directors shall be elected at the annual meeting of stockholders and each director shall be elected to serve until his successor shall be elected and shall qualify. The number of directors may not be less than three except that where all the shares of the corporation are owned beneficially and of record by either one or two stockholders, the number of directors may be less than three but not less than the number of stockholders.

SECTION 2. RESIGNATIONS. — Any director, member of a committee or other officer may resign at any time. Such resignation shall be made in writing, and shall take effect at the time specified therein, and if no time be specified, at the time of its receipt by the President or Secretary. The acceptance of a resignation shall not be necessary to make it effective.

SECTION 3. VACANCIES. — If the office of any director, member of a committee or other officer becomes vacant, the remaining directors in office, though less than a quorum by a majority vote, may appoint any qualified person to fill such vacancy, who shall hold office for the unexpired term and until his successor shall be duly chosen.

SECTION 4. REMOVAL. — Any director or directors may be removed either for or without cause at any time by the affirmative vote of the holders of majority of all the shares of stock outstanding and entitled to vote, at a special meeting of the stockholders called for the purpose and the vacancies thus created may be filled, at the meeting held for the purpose of removal, by the affirmative vote of a majority in interest of the stockholders entitled to vote.

SECTION 5. INCREASE OF NUMBER. — The number of directors may be increased by amendment of these By-Laws by the affirmative vote of a majority of the directors, though less than a quorum, or, by the affirmative vote of a majority in interest of the stockholders, at the annual meeting or at a special meeting called for that purpose, and by like vote the additional directors may be chosen at such meeting to hold office until the next annual election and until their successors are elected and qualify.

SECTION 6. COMPENSATION. — Directors shall not receive any stated salary for their services as directors or as members of committees, but by resolution of the board a fixed fee and expenses of attendance may be allowed for attendance at each meeting. Nothing herein contained shall be construed to preclude any director from serving the corporation in any other capacity as an officer, agent or otherwise, and receiving compensation thereof.

SECTION 7. ACTION WITHOUT MEETING. — Any action required or permitted to be taken at any meeting of the Board of Directors, or of any committee thereof, may be taken without a meeting, if prior of such action a written consent thereto is signed by all members of the board, or of such committee as the case may be, and such written consent is filed with the minutes of proceedings of the board or committee.

ARTICLE IV — OFFICERS

SECTION 1. OFFICERS. — The officers of the corporation shall consist of a President, a Treasurer, and a Secretary, and shall be elected by the Board of Directors and shall hold office until their successors are elected and qualified. In addition, the Board of Directors may elect a Chairman, one or more Vice-Presidents and such Assistant Secretaries and Assistant Treasurers as it may deem proper. None of the officers of the corporation need be directors. The officers shall be elected at the first meeting of the Board of Directors after each annual meeting. More than two offices may be held by the same person.

SECTION 2. OTHER OFFICERS AND AGENTS. — The Board of Directors may appoint such officers and agents as it may deem advisable, who shall hold their offices for such terms and shall exercise such power and perform such duties as shall be determined from time to time by the Board of Directors.

SECTION 3. CHAIRMAN. — The Chairman of the Board of Directors if one be elected, shall preside at all meetings of the Board of Directors, and he shall have and perform such other duties as from time to time may be assigned to him by the Board of Directors.

SECTION 4. PRESIDENT. — The President shall be the chief executive officer of the corporation and shall have the general powers and duties of supervision and management usually vested in the office of President of a corporation. He shall preside at all meetings of the stockholders if present thereat, and in the absence or non-election of the Chairman of the Board of Directors, at all meetings of the Board of Directors, and shall have general supervision, direction and control of the business of the corporation. Except as the Board of Directors shall authorize the execution thereof in some other manner, he shall execute bonds, mortgages, and other contracts in behalf of the corporation, and shall cause the seal to be affixed to any instrument requiring it, and when so affixed the seal shall be attested by the signature of the Secretary or the Treasurer or an Assistant Secretary or an Assistant Treasurer.

SECTION 5. VICE-PRESIDENT. — Each Vice-President shall have such powers and shall perform such duties as shall be assigned to him by the directors.

SECTION 6. TREASURER. — The Treasurer shall have the custody of the corporate funds and securities and shall keep full and accurate account of receipts and disbursements in books belonging to the corporation. He shall deposit all moneys and other valuables in the name and to the credit of the corporation in such depositories as may be designated by the Board of Directors.

The Treasurer shall disburse the funds of the corporation as may be ordered by the Board of Directors, or the President, taking proper vouchers for such disbursements. He shall render to the President and Board of Directors at the regular meetings of the Board of Directors, or whenever they may request it, an account of all his transactions as Treasurer and of the financial condition of the corporation. If required by the Board of Directors, he shall give the corporation a bond for the faithful discharge of his duties in such amount and with such surety as the board shall prescribe.

SECTION 7. SECRETARY. — The Secretary shall give, or cause to be given, notice of all meetings of stockholders and directors, and all other notices required by law or by these By-Laws, and in case of his absence or refusal or neglect to do so, any such notice may be given by any person thereunto directed by the President, or by the directors, or stockholders, upon whose requisition the meeting is called as provided in these By-Laws. He shall record all the proceedings of the meetings of the corporation and of directors in a book to be kept for that purpose and shall affix the seal to all instruments requiring it, when authorized by the directors or the President, and attest the same.

SECTION 8. ASSISTANT TREASURERS & ASSISTANT SECRETARIES. — Assistant Treasurers and Assistant Secretaries, if any, shall be elected and shall have such powers and shall perform such duties as shall be assigned to them, respectively, by the directors.

ARTICLE V

SECTION 1. CERTIFICATE OF STOCK. — Every holder of stock in the corporation shall be entitled to have a certificate, signed by, or in the name of the corporation by, the chairman or vice-chairman of the board of directors, or the president or a vice-president and the treasurer or an assistant treasurer, or the secretary of the corporation, certifying the number of shares owned by him in the corporation. If the corporation shall be authorized to issue more than one class of stock or more than one series of any class, the designations, preferences and relative, participating, optional or other special rights of each class of stock or series thereof, and the qualifications, limitations, or restrictions of such preferences and/or rights shall be set forth in full or summarized on the face or back of the certificate which the corporation shall issue to represent such class or series of stock, provided that, except as otherwise provided in section 202 of the General Corporation Law of Delaware in lieu of the foregoing requirements, there may be set forth on the face or back of the certificate which the corporation shall issue to represent such class or series of stock, a statement that the corporation will furnish without charge to each stockholder who so requests the powers, designations, preferences and relative, participating, optional or other special rights of each class of stock or series thereof and the qualifications, limitations or restrictions of such preferences and/or rights. Where a certificate is countersigned (1) by a transfer agent other than the corporation or its employee, or (2) by a registrar other than the corporation or its employee, the signatures of such officers may be facsimiles.

SECTION 2. LOST CERTIFICATES. — New certificates of stock may be issued in the place of any certificate therefore issued by the corporation, alleged to have been lost or destroyed, and the directors may, in their discretion, require the owner of the lost or destroyed certificate or his legal representatives, to give the corporation a bond, in such sum as they may direct, not exceeding double the value of the stock, to indemnify the corporation against it on account of alleged loss of any such new certificate.

SECTION 3. TRANSFER OF SHARES. — The shares of stock of the corporation shall be transferable only upon its books by the holders thereof in person or by their duly authorized attorneys or legal representatives, and upon such transfer the old certificates shall be surrendered to the corporation by the delivery thereof to the person in charge of the stock and transfer books and ledgers, or to such other persons as the directors may designate, by whom they shall be cancelled, and new certificates shall thereupon be issued. A record shall be made of each transfer and whenever a transfer shall be made for collateral security, and not absolutely, it shall be so expressed in the entry of the transfer.

SECTION 4. STOCKHOLDERS RECORDS DATE. — In order that the corporation may determine the stockholders entitled to notice of or to vote at any meeting of stockholders or any adjournment thereof, or to express consent to corporate action in writing without a meeting, or entitled to receive payment of any dividend or other distribution or allotment of any rights, or entitled to exercise any rights in respect of any change, conversion, or exchange of stock, or for the purpose of any other lawful action, the Board of Directors may fix, in advance, a record date, which shall not be more than sixty nor less than ten days before the day of such meeting, nor more than sixty days prior to any other action. A determination of stockholders of record entitled to notice of or to vote at a meeting of stockholders shall apply to any adjournment of the meeting provided, however, that the Board of Directors may fix a new record date for the adjourned meeting.

SECTION 5. DIVIDENDS. — Subject to the provisions of the Certificate of Incorporation the Board of Directors may, out of funds legally available therefor at any regular or special meeting, declare dividends upon the capital stock of the corporation as and when they deem expedient. Before declaring any dividends there may be set apart out of any funds of the corporation available for dividends, such sum or sums as the directors from time to time in their discretion deem proper working capital or as a reserve fund to meet contingencies or for equalizing dividends or for such other purposes as the directors shall deem conducive to the interests of the corporation.

SECTION 6. SEAL. — The corporate seal shall be circular in form and shall contain the name of the corporation, the year of its creation and the words "CORPORATE SEAL DELAWARE." Said seal may be used by causing it or a facsimile thereof to be impressed or affixed or otherwise reproduced.

SECTION 7. FISCAL YEAR. — The fiscal year of the corporation shall be determined by resolution of the Board of Directors.

SECTION 8. CHECKS. — All checks, drafts, or other orders for the payment of money, notes, or other evidences of indebtedness issued in the name of the corporation shall be signed by officer or officers, agent or agents of the corporation, and in such manner as shall be determined from time to time by resolution of the Board of Directors.

SECTION 9. NOTICE AND WAIVER OF NOTICE. — Whenever any notice is required by these By-Laws to be given, personal notice is not meant unless expressly stated, and any notice so required shall be deemed to be sufficient if given by depositing the same in the United States mail, postage prepaid, addressed to the person entitled thereto at his address as it appears on the records of the corporation, and such notice shall be deemed to have been given on the day of such mailing. Stockholders not entitled to vote shall not be entitled to receive notice of any meetings except as otherwise provided by statute.

Whenever any notice whatever is required to be given under the provisions of any law, or under the provisions of the Certificate of Incorporation of the corporation or these By-Laws, a waiver thereof in writing signed by the person or persons entitled to said notice, whether before or after the time stated therein, shall be deemed proper notice.

ARTICLE VI — AMENDMENTS

These By-Laws may be altered and repealed, and By-Laws may be made at any annual meeting of the stockholders or at any special meeting thereof if notice thereof is contained in the notice of such special meeting by the affirmative vote of a majority of the stock issued and outstanding or entitled to vote thereat, or by the regular meeting of the Board of Directors, if notice thereof is contained in the notice of such special meeting.

WHAT TO DO WHEN AN EXISTING ESTABLISHED BUSINESS INCORPORATES

SECTION XXII

There are some steps involved to transfer the financial records of a non-incorporated business to a corporation.

Below is a guideline to follow when a proprietorship or partnership becomes a corporation:

1. Arrange to form the corporation. If using a registered agent make this selection.

2. New books and records should be prepared to reflect the new corporate status and the corporation name.

    a. Decide whether to transfer accounts receivable* to the corporation and notify customers of the change. This is optional.

    b. Decide whether to transfer accounts payable* to the corporation and to notify creditors of the change.

    c. Decide whether to transfer capital assets* to the corporation.

    d. Decide whether to transfer inventory* to corporation records.

    e. Decide on the ending date of the corporate year to be used for income tax reporting purposes.

    f. Decide whether to notify all company associates and businesses dealt with as well as customers of the new corporate status. This can be done with sales producing advertising, and often, at no cost. Newspaper editors will usually run publicity of this new change on the financial page. An announcement by the owner(s) of the corporation should be typed and sent to the financial editor of the newspaper where the company's office is located.

3. Order new letterheads reflecting corporate name.

4. Open a bank account in the name of the corporation.

5. Transfer insurance policies to the corporation.

6. Arrange for any leases or other documents to be changed to reflect the corporation status.

7. Arrange to redo any employment contracts that exist with the old company, with the new corporation.

It would be helpful to counsel with an accountant and, if there are complications with agreements, with a lawyer on handling the above details.

---

* *If applicable.*

Slash Your Business Costs When You Join Entrepreneurs of America!

Entrepreneurs of America (EOA), a Business Resource Network serving small to medium-sized business owners nationwide offers big savings to you with a unique combination of benefits available only to its members.

The foundations of EOA were established 17 years ago when successful entrepreneur and best-selling author Ted Nicholas first began Enterprise Publishing, Inc. Today, the Network has grown to include a wide range of services, benefits, and support vital to the growth and prosperity of our membership.

If you already have an established business, or even if you are just thinking about starting one, we urge you to look at all that EOA can offer you in meeting your business needs.

EOA Membership Offers Big Savings On All Products/Services* You receive through the Resource Network

• Slash your cost of extending credit — immediately reduce your merchandise credit card processing fees on Visa and MasterCard to as low as 1.39% due to our special EOA group discount rates. No set up charges, and funds may be wired to your local bank within 48 hours, depending on the type of processing you choose.

• Receive a 20% or more discount on resources including books, periodicals and other business products.

• Incorporate in 11 minutes or less by telephone. Just choose the name and call. Your cost is only $85. (Over the past 17 years, we have incorporated over 70,000 companies using this method.)

• Save on Safeguard Business Recordkeeping systems. As a member of EOA you are entitled to a special 10% savings off Safeguard systems for checkwriting, invoicing, payroll and many other accounting functions. (This exclusive EOA offer is available only to new Safeguard customers and may not be used in combination with any other promotional offer.)

• EOA/Ask Mr. Foster Travel Program with guaranteed lowest travel fares and discounted hotel and motel rates.

• EOA Gold MasterCard for business or personal use that begins with the first six months free and offers a low introductory interest rate of just 12%.

• The opportunity to invest in gold and other precious metals with no sales tax . . . a savings of 8% or more depending on your location.

• A free subscription to *ENTREPRENEURS OF AMERICA* Newsletter which will keep you current on the entire Resource Network as well as other vital matters affecting your business interests.

• Lobbying in Washington on matters generally affecting small businesses is an ongoing benefit that is provided as part of your EOA membership.

In addition to all of these great and growing benefits, we have a network of over 250 lobbyists. These former Senators, Congressmen, and others experienced in state and federal lobbying are available at discounted rates to you as a member of EOA for your specific needs. No other small business organization we know offers such a powerful resource!

EOA Supports All Phases of Your Business Life Cycle

The EOA Resource Network understands that the concerns and needs of an emerging entrepreneur are very different from those of an established and thriving business owner. Therefore, our information and support services have been specifically designed to correspond with the 4 major phases of the business life cycle. This structuring of the vast resources available through the Network has helped make information easier to locate and tap by our members.

Which of These 4 Stages Fits You?

I. Emerging Entrepreneur — Individuals engaged in planning and determining the feasibility of a business.

II. The Growing Business — The first two critical years when a business is launched and may be succeeding but is not yet profitable.

III. The Maturing Business — Companies that have survived the treacherous first two years, but still have not reached the five year mark.

IV. The Established Entrepreneur — Individuals that have been in business five-plus years, managing successfully.

Special Bonus —Yours FREE!

If you enroll now, we will send you absolutely free a copy of *Management for Entrepreneurs* by Ted Nicholas, ($29.95 value). Based on Nicholas's own successful experiences as a business owner, this book shows any manager, particularly in a small business, how to create an effective, profitable organization.

Satisfaction Guaranteed

Let us prove the value of the EOA Business Resource Network. As a member, you take no risk whatsoever. If you are not delighted in every way, you will receive a prompt and courteous refund of your membership fee upon request.

Join EOA now. Membership is just $49.95 (tax deductible). You'll see that it's a great way to help you start a business, or make your ongoing venture grow and prosper!

For fastest service, call toll-free:
1-800-533-2665.
Or, complete the form below and mail.

Terms and conditions of any EOA membership program are subject to change without notice.

© 1990 Entrepreneurs Of America   O-1010

How to Get Your Own Trademark and Protect Your Single Most Important Asset — Your Good Name

Discover step-by-step how easily you can do it yourself and save a fortune in legal fees. New book includes ready to use tear-out forms for everything you need.

The single most important asset of your business is the good name attached to your products and services.

If you have name recognition, customers will seek out that product or service by name. And that name may be of immeasurable value, even worth millions, in the form of goodwill should you ever decide to sell your business.

The safest, most effective way to protect a name is to obtain a *federal trademark*. You then are in the best position to guard against strangers usurping your name.

What is a trademark? It may be a word, symbol, design, or combined word and design, or a slogan. Or even a distinctive sound. When used to identify a product, the mark is known as a trademark. When used to identify a service, the mark is termed a service mark.

Once your name is embraced by trademark protection, it can remain yours forever. All you need to do is use it and renew it every twenty years to protect it. You thus retain the exclusive right to that name in perpetuity.

A new book has just been completed that provides all the information you need. *How To Get Your Own Trademark* is the title. The purpose of this essential book from the editors of Enterprise Publishing is to show you:

1. Why you and/or your business should obtain trademark protection
2. How easy and inexpensive it can be for you to obtain that protection yourself, without engaging costly legal or other professional assistance
3. The simple, straightforward steps you can take to insure that once you obtain trademark protection, it's yours for as long as you want it.

All the forms and documents you need to obtain trademark registration are contained in the book. The procedures you should follow to keep that protection in force are also described.

A word of warning. Many people believe that they have obtained name protection for their company when they incorporated. Not true. Other people can legally use your name in other states in which you are *not* incorporated, and, if they file for trademark protection, you will be out in the cold. In that case, you will have to go through the expense and hassle of changing the name. The book shows how to conduct a low cost name search to avoid problems initially.

Of course, even if your corporate name is covered by a trademark, you still need to cover any special product or service names you may have developed. Otherwise, you will be using an unprotected name that someone else can legally use.

What You Can Register as a Trademark

1. **Words.** A. Coined words. Examples include *Kodak, Exxon, Pyrex* and *Sunoco*
   B. Suggestive words. For example, *BAN* deodorant
   C. Dictionary words. For example, *Apple* Computer
2. **Designs.** Such as, the *golden arches* of the *McDonald Corporation*
3. **Initials or Numbers.** Examples, *IBM, 3M* and *AT&T*
4. **Slogans.** For example, *"There's a Ford in Your Future"*
5. **Labels.** Uniquely distinctive designs such as *Smuckers* Jellies
6. **Container and Building Designs.** For example, the *Coca Cola* bottle, the pinch bottle for *Haig & Haig Scotch* or the *Fotomat* structures
7. **Certification and Collective Marks.** For example, *"Underwriters Laboratories"*

The book shows you:

- how to get a trademark search done at low cost
- what to do if someone is infringing on your trademark
- what to do if your trademark application is denied. Yes, you can fight if you are turned down, and win!
- how to get trademark protection in other countries
- how to comply with trademark registration, with complete step by step instructions
- how to use the trademark application forms provided for an individual, partnership or corporation, complete with samples and tear-out forms
- how to write a letter confronting any infringer of your trademark

If you want trademark protection or are considering it. *How to Get Your Own Trademark* is <u>must</u> reading. Order your copy today.

Money back guarantee

If for any reason after examining the book for 30 days you are not delighted, you may return it for a prompt and courteous refund.

To order your copy, call now toll free: **1-800-533-2665** or complete coupon below and mail.

This offering is endorsed by the **Entrepreneurs of America**. EOA members are entitled to a 20% courtesy discount on books and other benefits. For complete membership information, call the EOA at **1-800-533-2665**.

© 1990 Enterprise Publishing, Inc.   N-1010

What Will You Do When Your Personal Assets Are Seized to Satisfy A Judgment Against Your Corporation?

All your many tax benefits of owning a corporation could be wiped out overnight. How? The I.R.S. could visit you and claim you have not kept proper corporate minutes. You could lose the very tax benefits to which the law entitles you.

Here are some recent "horror stories" direct from actual court cases:

Joseph P. obtained a loan from his corporation without the proper loan documents and corporate minutes. As a result, the court required him to pay additional taxes of $27,111.60. He narrowly escaped a penalty of $13,555.80.

B.W.C., Inc. was forced to pay $106,358.61 of accumulated earnings tax because its corporate minutes were incomplete. They expressed "no specific, definite, or feasible plans" to justify accumulating earnings, according to the court.

Keeping records has always been a bother, and an expensive one, especially for small companies. Most entrepreneurs do not like to spend time keeping records. Probably because no one ever became rich by keeping records. And in a small, one-person business, it seems downright silly to keep records of stockholder meetings and board of directors meetings . . . keeping minutes . . . taking votes . . . adopting resolutions . . . isn't it all just a waste of time?

Not if you ask any of the thousands of entrepreneurs who have lost fortunes because they failed to keep records. You should look at corporate record keeping chores this way: *It's part of the price you pay to get the tax benefits and personal protection from having a corporation.*

A corporation does not exist except on paper, through its charter, by-laws, stock certificates, resolutions, etc. Anything you do as an officer or director has to be duly authorized and evidenced by a resolution of the stockholders or the board, or by both in some cases. It makes no difference if there is only one stockholder or one million stockholders. The rules are basically the same.

You can hire a lawyer, like the big companies do, and pay $100 or more just to prepare one form. But you may need, at minimum, a dozen or more documents to keep your corporation alive and functioning for just one year. This type of work is the bread and butter for many corporation lawyers. Most of the work can be done by their secretaries, yet they will charge you enormous sums because they know how important these forms are.

There is now a way for you to solve your

© 1990 Enterprise Publishing, Inc.

corporate recordkeeping problems. Without a lawyer, without paying big fees, and without spending a lot of time. Virtually all the forms you will ever need are already compiled in **The Complete Book of Corporate Forms** by Ted Nicholas. Nicholas also wrote the best-seller, *How To Form Your Own Corporation Without A Lawyer For Under $50.* This book has become the largest single source of new corporations in America and has revolutionized the business of forming new corporations by making the process simple, easy and inexpensive.

But forming a corporation is only the first step toward building "the ultimate tax shelter." Through carelessness or neglect, many people are denied their rightful benefits from owning their own corporation. Ted Nicholas saw that many business owners needed more help *after* they incorporated.

And so, he prepared **The Complete Book of Corporate Forms.** Everything is simplified. Either you or your secretary can complete any form in minutes. All you do is fill in a few blanks and insert the completed form in your record book. When you own this book, you are granted permission to reproduce every form. If you are behind on keeping your corporate records, now you can catch up in no time. Just complete a few blanks for the things you've already done in the company. It's legal and it works. Best of all, the price is less than you would pay a lawyer for one hour of counseling.

Here is just a sampling of what you'll receive:

Minutes of Stockholder Meetings
Minutes of Directors Meetings
Minutes of Special Meetings

(Any of these can be used if you are the only stockholder and director.)
Amendments to Articles of Incorporation
Amendments to By-Laws
Changes in Membership of Board

You will also receive all the stockholder and directors resolutions you will need, including:

• Negotiations of contracts • Authorizing loans to corporation • Approval of corporate loans to you • Designation of purchasing agent *(some suppliers may want to know who is authorized to buy from them)* • Setting your salary • Directors fees • Authorizing your expense account • Mergers • Sale of corporate assets • Dissolution • Bankruptcy • Declaring dividends • Appointment of attorney or accountant

Plus, you'll receive the forms needed to authorize any of these tax-saving fringe benefits:

• Pension or profit-sharing plans • Medical and dental reimbursement plans • Sick pay plans • Split dollar life insurance • Educational loan program • Scholarship aid program • Stock options • Group life insurance • Financial counseling plan • Group legal services • Christmas bonus, special bonuses

Just one of the above forms can cost you hundreds of dollars in legal fees . . .

This entire 8½ x 11, loose leaf collection of simplified forms, (over 150 pages of forms), with clear instructions for their use, as well as samples of completed forms, sells for only $49.95

And, as with all Enterprise Publishing products, it sells under an iron-clad 30-day money-back guarantee. Examine the collection, and if for any reason you are not pleased, return it for a prompt refund. Take a moment to place your order now, and immediately begin saving time and money. Complete coupon and mail.

SUGGESTED READINGS

SECTION XXIII

A list of some of the author's other books as well as favorite readings are included. Some titles have little to do with incorporating but are included as aids to thinking. Others are oriented toward business. Still others are philosophical or psychological in nature. All are suggested aids to thinking, self-improvement, or formulating business ideas.

Caples, John, MAKING ADS PAY.
  Dover Press, New York, New York

Editors at Enterprise, EXECUTIVE'S BUSINESS LETTER BOOK.
  Enterprise Publishing, Inc., Wilmington, Delaware

Friedman, Robert, SMALL BUSINESS LEGAL HANDBOOK.
  Enterprise Publishing, Inc., Wilmington, Delaware

Goldstein, Arnold S., BASIC BOOK OF BUSINESS AGREEMENTS.
  Enterprise Publishing, Inc., Wilmington, Delaware

Goldstein, Arnold S., COMPLETE CREDIT AND COLLECTION SYSTEM.
  Enterprise Publishing, Inc., Wilmington, Delaware

Goldstein, Arnold S., and Peter Knox, THE COMPLETE BOOK OF CORPORATE BENEFITS.
  Enterprise Publishing, Inc., Wilmington, Delaware

Goldstein, Arnold S., COMPLETE BOOK OF EMPLOYEE FORMS.
  Enterprise Publishing, Inc., Wilmington, Delaware

Goldstein, Arnold S., DIRECTOR'S PORTFOLIO.
  Enterprise Publishing, Inc., Wilmington, Delaware

Grant, Richard W., THE INCREDIBLE BREAD MACHINE.
  Academic Associates, Los Angeles, California

Nicholas, Ted, COMPLETE NON-PROFIT CORPORATION HANDBOOK.
  Enterprise Publishing, Inc., Wilmington, Delaware

Nicholas, Ted, THE GOLDEN MAILBOX.
  Enterprise Publishing, Inc., Wilmington, Delaware

Nicholas, Ted, THE S CORPORATION HANDBOOK.
  Enterprise Publishing, Inc., Wilmington, Delaware

Nicholas, Ted, TED NICHOLAS SMALL BUSINESS COURSE.
  Enterprise Publishing, Inc., Wilmington, Delaware

Nicholas, Ted, THE COMPLETE BOOK OF CORPORATE FORMS.
  Enterprise Publishing, Inc., Wilmington, Delaware

Rand, Ayn, ATLAS SHRUGGED.
  Random House, New York, New York

Rand, Ayn, CAPITALISM: THE UNKNOWN IDEAL.
  Signal Books, The New American Library, New York, New York

A few of the Companies that have already incorporated through this book —
From all 50 States and other countries throughout the world.

Name	Type of Business
AIDA Group Travel Coordinators & Travel Agents, Inc.	Group and individual travel to the general public
Airspeed Refinishing, Inc.	Custom painting of aircraft and other vehicles
Alaska Book Company	Book Sales
Allied Auto International, Ltd.	Services and delivery of foreign vehicles to U.S.A.
Amazing Diets, Inc.	Publishers
American Armed Forces Association	Fraternal servicemen's organization
The American Society of Child Advocates	Non-profit society to promote children's rights
Arundel Pool Management, Inc.	Management, opening, closing and maintenance of swimming pools
Balancing Act Corporation	Manufacture of weighing scales
The Balloon Company	Operate a balloon for hire
Better Builders & Remodelers, Inc.	Building and remodeling of residential and commercial buildings
Better Business Maintenance Co.	Janitorial and maintenance services
Bost Farms, Inc.	Farming
Calphil Corporation	Import-Export
Chronos, Incorporated	Financial Planning
Cicero Cheese Manufacturing Corp.	Manufacture of cheese
Cindex Incorporated	Computer technical services
Covered Bridge Craft Barn and Garden Centre, Incorporated	Retail and wholesale sales of crafts, antiques, and plants through garden center
Creative Products, Inc.	Marketing organization
Criminal Justice Associates, Inc.	Consultations to Criminal Justice schools and agencies
The Cron Corporation	Printing, publishing and management services
Cultural Commercial Exchange, Inc.	Cultural/commercial centers and festival sponsorship
Dakota Nomad, Inc.	Bicycle and cross-country ski retail sales and manufacture of accessories
Denticare of Delaware, Inc.	Prepaid dental healthcare plan
Dexterity Unlimited, Inc.	Retail and wholesale sales and production of handcrafted items
Different Drummer, Inc.	Yacht charter
The Dinky Rink, Inc.	Roller skating
Doug's Aircraft Interiors, Inc.	Aircraft upholstery and accessories
Electron Optics Corporation	Manufacturing of surveillance equipment
Energy Independence Now, Inc.	Alternative energy sources
Eunitron, Inc.	Provide investment advisory service (publish a market letter)
European Overseas American, Inc.	Banking abroad, merchant banking
Excelsior International Corporation	Import and export
Fallbrook Ranchers, Inc.	Avocado and josoba nut ranching
Family Name Researchers, Inc.	Researching of surnames, family trees, genealogy, production of armorial bearings, etc.
Finance Corporation for Credit & Commerce	Financial and investment services
Flash Clinic Inc.	Service and repair of electronic flash equipment
Garon Enterprises, Inc.	Numismatics
Golconda Feed & Grain, Inc.	Agricultural products
Green Cargo, Inc.	Diversified sales of plants and accessories
Group Two, Inc.	Educational Seminars
The Growing Concern, Inc.	Greenhouses, solar systems
Guardian Protective Coatings, Inc.	Applications and sales of protective coatings
Honey Creek Farm, Inc.	Livestock farming
Hypertension Clinic, Inc.	Medical and health care, and teaching
Imperial Adhesives, Ltd.	Light manufacturing
Infinity's Child, Inc.	Decorating glass
Institute for Neuropsychopharmacologic Research, Inc.	Scientific research

Name	Type of Business
International Development Service Corp.	Export/import trade
International Geophysics, Inc.	Geophysical sales and services
Jetair, Inc.	Dealers in aircraft, flight instruction, and general aviation services
K & B Sink Tops, Inc.	Manufacturer of sink and counter tops
The Lighthouse Repertory Theatre, Inc.	Theatrical productions
Mafia, Inc.	Bumper stickers
Mountain Sales, Inc.	Redwood table sales (handmade)
Music Makers Unlimited, Inc.	Musical services, band and orchestra
Nova Hang Gliders, Inc.	Sales and service of hang gliders and accessories
OMV Corporation	Real estate
Old Worlds Antiques Corporation	Wholesale and retail antiques
PeTaxi, Inc.	Rescue, receiving, air-shipping of pets, pet sitting, escort service for housepets
Pickwick Enterprises Corporation	Fish & Chips shop
Pineville Medical Clinic, Inc.	Health and medical service
Plane, Inc.	Transportation
Psychynotics Foundation	Research and teaching of hypnosis, mind control metaphysics, psychic phenomena
R and B Logging, Inc.	Timber logging
Rainsong Institute	Advocacy of efficient energy use
Red Dawn Productions, Inc.	Film Production
Reel Creations, Inc.	Music
Regina Careers, Ltd.	Self-training courses for home study
Scientific Resumes, Inc.	Polygraph testing
Seaboard Resources, Inc.	Management consulting and trading
Sign of the Times Corporation	Silk-screened garments
Simmons Industries, Inc.	Design, development, manufacture and sales of poultry processing and related equipment and supplies
Snowcrest Corp.	Horsebreeding and training
Sponsler-Nitrogen-Service, Inc.	Retail — fertilizer, chemicals and apply same
Stock Shot Corporation	Marketing curling and skiing equipment
Tectonics International, Inc.	Architecture, engineering, construction, development, and management services in U.S. and abroad
Texmark Corporation	Act as holding company for retail and wholesale operations of liquor and supermarkets, brewing industry
The Thomas Talin Company	Fragrance
Thor-Bred Health Food Corporation	Health food for thoroughbred horses and other animals
To Have and To Hold Shops, Inc.	Misses sportswear
Transcontinental International, Inc.	Coal and energy products, sales and production
Transprocess Manufacturing Marketing Support Corporation	Business, tax and economy advices
Undersea Life Sciences Corp.	Consulting services for diving/hyperbaric related industries
Union-Euro-Market, Inc.	Investments
Virginia Pork Corporation	Commercial swine production
Whitehouse Foods, Inc.	Retail Grocery Store
Woodcat Investments, Inc.	Investments
World Amateur Backgammon Championships, Inc.	Promotion of backgammon and other tournaments
World Backgammon Federation, Inc.	Sanctioning body for backgammon tournaments and official players and promoters organization
World Business Investment, Inc.	Real estate investment, sales and business opportunities
World Cycle, Inc.	Motorcycle repair and sales
Xanthippe Corp.	Investments
Zoii, Inc.	Natural clothing, crafts, etc.

Notes

Notes

Notes

Notes

Notes

Notes

Notes

Notes

Notes

Notes

Notes

Notes

Notes